POETRY OF LOVE FOR EVERY DAY
OF THE YEAR

POETRY OF LOVE FOR EVERY DAY OF THE YEAR

EDITED BY
JANE McMORLAND HUNTER

BATSFORD

DEDICATION

To John, Tabitha and Matilda, with all my love, for ever.

First published in the United Kingdom
in 2024 by
Batsford
43 Great Ormond Street
London
WC1N 3HZ

An imprint of B. T. Batsford Holdings Limited

Copyright © B. T. Batsford Ltd, 2024

All rights reserved. No part of this publication may be copied, displayed, extracted, reproduced, utilized, stored in a retrieval system or transmitted in any form or by any means, electronic, mechanical or otherwise including but not limited to photocopying, recording, or scanning without the prior written permission of the publishers.

ISBN 9781849949163

A CIP catalogue record for this book is available from the British Library.

10 9 8 7 6 5 4 3 2 1

Reproduction by Rival Colour Ltd, UK
Printed by Dream Colour, China

This book can be ordered direct from the publisher at www.batsfordbooks.com, or try your local bookshop

CONTENTS

JANUARY 10
With a Smile

FEBRUARY 46
If We're Together

MARCH 82
Look in Thy Heart

APRIL 120
What Joys Exceeding

MAY 154
Trust All to Love

JUNE 190
All Thoughts, All Passions

JULY 226
Two Hearts Beating

AUGUST 266
To Sit and Dream

SEPTEMBER 302
A Thrill in My Heart

OCTOBER 340
Gathered to Thy Heart

NOVEMBER 376
Life of My Life

DECEMBER 412
Thy Heart is Mine

INDEX OF FIRST LINES 448
INDEX OF POETS 461
SOURCES 470

Introduction

Poets have probably written about love, in all its guises, more than any other subject. First love, unrequited love, true, false, found or lost – love, or its absence, appears in verse throughout history. Everyone experiences love, or the lack of it, regardless of the times in which they live or their social standing.

Poets such as William Shakespeare and Elizabeth Barratt Browning have attempted to find a definition but, despite their vast output, neither really succeeded. The simple phrases 'I am in love' or 'I love you' encompass a huge range of emotions, different for almost every person who thinks or utters them. The protagonists here range from knights and kings to shepherds and the enslaved, happily married couples to scoundrels and rogues. In compiling this anthology, I have attempted to include poems that cover all aspects of love poetry, although I have largely avoided the overtly suicidal or sexual.

The protective love of a parent or older sibling is the earliest love addressed by most poets, with George Eliot's little girl blindly following her adored older brother. Then there is the first or true love, one that can set the pattern for the rest of a life, even though we may not recognize this at the time or even remember the event in detail, 'So unrecorded did it slip away, / So blind was I to see and to foresee,' (Christina Rossetti). With luck, at least in poetry, one finds a soul mate such as Robert Burns' John Anderson. According to some poets, we should 'Gather ye Rose-buds while ye may' or 'go no more a roving' in old age, but for others age is no bar to love; they are kissed and loved even when ancient. Finally, there is love that continues after death. Some people cannot live contentedly without their beloved, following them swiftly to the grave, some mourn patiently while others start again.

Between these pages there is a wide range of emotions: spurned lovers (Brian Bilston), unrealistic optimists (Robert Graves) or those who missed their chance. Here we have to feel sorry for Thomas Hardy, or at least his subjects, who fail to leap off a train in search of love and, later in this anthology, fail to take advantage of a timely thunderstorm. Poems about animals are included in this collection, both our love for them and theirs for us or each other. Nature too is included, bringing inspiration or solace. There are different reasons for love including diamonds, a peerage and hard cash, but one would like to think such materialistic aims are in the minority; I have certainly arranged this collection to make this so.

Many of these poems tell stories, offer advice or give warnings; there is a learned lady disappointed by her worldly spouse, several plans to marry and a knight who has been tragically seduced by a faery. Gifts are given, declarations made and, on at least two occasions, stark warnings offered regarding the pitfalls of marriage; it seems charming women and most men are best avoided! Some, though, ignore all the advice and a young subaltern and a girl with six interfering relatives happily aim to tie the knot. Love may be a serious business, but many poets also see the funny side: the loss of the corkscrew may be more keenly felt than that of the lover, and advice can be twisted, on being told he should find a wife, one young man asks whose wife he should take.

    I have deliberately not followed any path in this anthology; each poem stands alone and, if anything, is placed to contrast with its neighbours rather than directly connect with them. I wanted to create a sense of the vastness of the subject, with love as something infinitely variable. For this reason, I have included over two hundred poets spanning more than six hundred years and circling the globe. Love may be impossible to define accurately, but that does not make it any less welcome or important to everyone.

It may well be that in a difficult hour,
Pinned down by pain and moaning for release,
Or nagged by want past resolution's power,
I might be driven to sell your love for peace,
Or trade the memory of this night for food.
It may well be. I do not think I would.

Edna St Vincent Millay from *Sonnet XXX*

JANUARY

With a Smile

1 JANUARY

Sonnet 116

Let me not to the marriage of true minds
Admit impediments. Love is not love
Which alters when it alteration finds,
Or bends with the remover to remove:
O, no! it is an ever-fixèd mark,
That looks on tempests and is never shaken;
It is the star to every wandering bark,
Whose worth's unknown, although his height be taken.
Love's not time's fool, though rosy lips and cheeks
Within his bending sickle's compass come;
Love alters not with his brief hours and weeks,
But bears it out even to the edge of doom.
   If this be error, and upon me proved,
   I never writ, nor no man ever loved.

William Shakespeare (1564–1616)

2 JANUARY

Early Affection

I loved thee from the earliest dawn,
   When first I saw thy beauty's ray;
And will until life's eve comes on,
   And beauty's blossom fades away;
And when all things go well with thee,
With smiles or tears remember me.

I'll love thee when thy morn is past
   And wheedling galantry is o'er,
When youth is lost in age's blast,
   And beauty can ascend no more;
And when life's journey ends with thee,
O then look back and think of me.

I'll love thee with a smile or frown,
   Mid sorrow's gloom or pleasure's light;
And when the chain of life runs down,
   Pursue thy last eternal flight;
When thou hast spread thy wing to flee,
Still, still a moment wait for me.

I love thee for those sparkling eyes,
   To which my fondness was betray'd,
Bearing the tincture of the skies,
   To glow when other beauties fade;
And when they sink too low to see,
Reflect an azure beam on me.

George Moses Horton (1798–c. 1883)

3 JANUARY

She Tells Her Love While Half Asleep

She tells her love while half asleep,
  In the dark hours,
    With half-words whispered low:
As Earth stirs in her winter sleep
  And put out grass and flowers
    Despite the snow,
    Despite the falling snow.

Robert Graves (1895–1985)

4 JANUARY

Air

FROM *A NEW CANTATA*

Wou'd you wish to keep your lover,
   Lay these wanton airs aside;
Do not all your charms discover,
   Let discretion be your guide.

When the object is deserving,
   And your heart declares for one;
All your charms for him reserving,
   Should the rest he reigns alone.

Smiles and looks to all imparted,
   Have no value, no regard,
But to be by all deserted,
   Is the vain Coquette's reward.

Clara Reeve (1729–1807)

5 JANUARY

Without Ceremony

It was your way, my dear,
To be gone without a word
When callers, friends, or kin
Had left, and I hastened in
To rejoin you, as I inferred.

And when you'd a mind to career
Off anywhere – say to town –
You were all on a sudden gone
Before I had thought thereon,
Or noticed your trunks were down.

So, now that you disappear
For ever in that swift style,
Your meaning seems to me
Just as it used to be:
'Good-bye is not worth while!'

Thomas Hardy (1840–1928)

6 JANUARY

Love

Love is like a lamb, and love is like a lion;
Fly from love, he fights, fight, then does he fly on;
Love is all in fire, and yet is ever freezing;
Love is much in winning, yet is more in leezing;
Love is ever sick, and yet is never dying;
Love is ever true, and yet is ever lying;
Love does dote in liking, and is mad in loathing;
Love indeed is anything, yet indeed is nothing.

Thomas Middleton (1580–1627)

7 JANUARY

I wish I could remember

'ERA GIÀ L'ORA CHE VOLGE IL DESIO.' – DANTE
'RICORRO AL TEMPO CH'IO VI VIDI PRIMA.' – PETRARCA
FROM *MONNA INNOMINATA: A SONNET OF SONNETS*

I wish I could remember that first day,
   First hour, first moment of your meeting me,
   If bright or dim the season, it might be
Summer or Winter for aught I can say;
So unrecorded did it slip away,
   So blind was I to see and to foresee,
   So dull to mark the budding of my tree
That would not blossom yet for many a May.
If only I could recollect it, such
   A day of days! I let it come and go
   As traceless as a thaw of bygone snow;
It seemed to mean so little, meant so much;
If only now I could recall that touch,
   First touch of hand in hand – Did one but know!

Christina Rossetti (1830–1894)

8 January

A Poet to His Beloved

I bring you with reverent hands
The books of my numberless dreams,
White woman that passion has worn
As the tide wears the dove-grey sands,
And with heart more old than the horn
That is brimmed from the pale fire of time:
White woman with numberless dreams,
I bring you my passionate rhyme.

W. B. Yeats (1865–1939)

9 JANUARY

Edward III

FROM ACT I, SCENE I

Enter Gaveston reading a letter that was bought him from the King.

Gaveston:
'My father is deceas'd. Come, Gaveston,
And share the kingdom with thy dearest friend.'
Ah, words that make me surfeit with delight!
What greater bliss can hap to Gaveston
Than live and be the favourite of a king?
Sweet prince, I come! these, these thy amorous lines
Might have enforc'd me to have swum from France,
And, like Leander, gasp'd upon the sand,
So thou wouldst smile, and take me in thine arms.
The sight of London to my exil'd eyes
Is as Elysium to a new-come soul:
Not that I love the city or the men,
But that it harbours him I hold so dear,
The king, upon whose bosom let me lie,
And with the world be still at enmity.
What need the arctic people love star-light,
To whom the sun shines both by day and night?
Farewell base stooping to the lordly peers;
My knee shall bow to none but to the king.

Christopher Marlowe (1564-1593)

10 JANUARY

4

FROM *THE DREAM SONGS*

Filling her compact & delicious body
with chicken páprika, she glanced at me
twice.
Fainting with interest, I hungered back
and only the fact of her husband & four other people
kept me from springing on her

or falling at her little feet and crying
'You are the hottest one for years of night
Henry's dazed eyes
have enjoyed, Brilliance.' I advanced upon
(despairing) my spumoni.—Sir Bones: is stuffed,
de world, wif feeding girls.

—Black hair, complexion Latin, jewelled eyes
downcast . . . The slob beside her   feasts . . . What
    wonders is
she sitting on, over there?
The restaurant buzzes. She might as well be on Mars.
Where did it all go wrong? There ought to be a law
    against Henry.
—Mr. Bones: there is.

John Berryman (1914–1972)

11 JANUARY

A Woman's Answer

I will not let you say a Woman's part
   Must be to give exclusive love alone;
Dearest, although I love you so, my heart
   Answers a thousand claims beside your own.

I love – what do I not love? earth and air
   Find space within my heart, and myriad things
You would not deign to heed, are cherished there,
   And vibrate on its very inmost strings.

I love the summer with her ebb and flow
   Of light, and warmth, and music that have nurst
Her tender buds to blossoms . . . and you know
   It was in summer that I saw you first.

I love the winter dearly too, . . . but then
   I owe it so much; on a winter's day,
Bleak, cold, and stormy, you returned again,
   When you had been those weary months away.

I love the Stars like friends; so many nights
   I gazed at them, when you were far from me,
Till I grew blind with tears . . . those far-off lights
   Could watch you, whom I longed in vain to see.

I love the Flowers; happy hours lie
   Shut up within their petals close and fast:
You have forgotten, dear: but they and I
   Keep every fragment of the golden Past.

I love, too, to be loved; all loving praise
    Seems like a crown upon my Life, – to make
It better worth the giving, and to raise
    Still nearer to your own the heart you take.

I love all good and noble souls; – I heard
    One speak of you but lately, and for days
Only to think of it, my soul was stirred
    In tender memory of such generous praise.

I love all those who love you; all who owe
    Comfort to you: and I can find regret
Even for those poorer hearts who once could know,
    And once could love you, and can now forget.

Well, is my heart so narrow – I, who spare
    Love for all these? Do I not even hold
My favourite books in special tender care,
    And prize them as a miser does his gold?

The Poets that you used to read to me
    While summer twilights faded in the sky;
But most of all I think Aurora Leigh,
    Because – because – do you remember why?

Will you be jealous? Did you guess before
    I loved so many things? – Still you the best: –
Dearest, remember that I love you more,
    Oh, more a thousand times than all the rest!

Adelaide Procter (1825–1864)

12 JANUARY

Air VIII

FROM *THE BEGGAR'S OPERA*, ACT II, SCENE VIII

Polly:
Can love be controlled by advice?
   Will Cupid our mothers obey?
Though my heart were as frozen as ice,
   As his flame 'twould have melted away.
When he kissed me, so closely he pressed,
   'Twas so sweet that I must have complied;
So I thought it both safest and best
   To marry, for fear you should chide.

John Gay (1685–1732)

13 JANUARY

A Soldier's Kiss

Only a dying horse! pull off the gear,
And slip the needless bit from frothing jaws,
Drag it aside there, leaving the road way clear,
The battery thunders on with scarce a pause.

Prone by the shell-swept highway there it lies
With quivering limbs, as fast the life-tide fails,
Dark films are closing o'er the faithful eyes
That mutely plead for aid where none avails.

Onward the battery rolls, but one there speeds
Heedlessly of comrades voices or bursting shell,
Back to the wounded friend who lonely bleeds
Beside the stony highway where he fell.

Only a dying horse! he swiftly kneels,
Lifts the limp head and hears the shivering sigh
Kisses his friend, while down his cheek there steals
Sweet pity's tear, "Goodbye old man, Goodbye".

No honours wait him, medal, badge or star,
Though scarce could war a kindlier deed unfold;
He bears within his breast, more precious far
Beyond the gift of kings, a heart of gold.

Henry Chappell (1874–1937)

14 JANUARY

A Face that should content me wonders well

A face that should content me wonders well,
   Should not be faire but lovelie to behold,
With gladsome cheare all grief for to expell;
   With sober lookes so wold I that it should
Speake without wordes, such woordes as non can tell;
   The tresse also should be of crysped gold.
With witt: and thus might chance I might be tyde,
   And knyt agayne the knott that should not slide.

Sir Thomas Wyatt (1503–1542)

15 JANUARY

An Arundel Tomb

Side by side, their faces blurred,
The earl and countess lie in stone,
Their proper habits vaguely shown
As jointed armour, stiffened pleat,
And that faint hint of the absurd –
The little dog under their feet.

Such plainness of the pre-baroque
Hardly involves the eye, until
It meets his left-hand gauntlet, still
Clasped empty in the other; and
One sees, with a sharp tender shock,
His hand withdrawn, holding her hand.

They would not think to lie so long.
Such faithfulness in effigy
Was just a detail friends would see:
A sculptor's sweet commissioned grace
Thrown off in helping to prolong
The Latin names around the base.

They would not guess how early in
Their supine stationary voyage
The air would change to soundless damage,
Turn the tenantry away;
How soon succeeding eyes begin
To look, not read. Rigidly they

Persisted, linked, through lengths and breadths
Of time. Snow fell, undated. Light
Each summer thronged the glass. A bright
Litter of birdcalls strewed the same
Bone-riddled ground. And up the paths
The endless altered people came,

Washing at their identity.
Now, helpless in the hollow of
An unarmorial age, a trough
Of smoke in slow suspended skeins
Above their scrap of history,
Only an attitude remains:

Time has transfigured them into
Untruth. The stone fidelity
They hardly meant has come to be
Their final blazon, and to prove
Our almost-instinct almost true:
What will survive of us is love.

Philip Larkin (1922–1985)

16 JANUARY

To a Wandering Female Singer

Thou hast loved and thou hast suffer'd!
   Unto feeling deep and strong,
Thou hast trembled like a harp's frail string –
   I know it by thy song!

Thou hast loved – it may be vainly –
   But well – oh! but too well –
Thou hast suffer'd all that woman's breast
   May bear – but must not tell.

Thou hast wept and thou hast parted.
   Thou hast been forsaken long.
Thou hast watch'd for steps that came not back –
   I know it by thy song!

By the low clear silvery gushing
   Of its music from thy breast.
By the quivering of its flute-like swell –
   A sound of the heart's unrest.

By its fond and plaintive lingering.
   On each word of grief so long.
Oh! thou hast loved and suffer'd much –
   I know it by thy song!

Felicia Hemans (1793–1835)

17 JANUARY

That I did always love

That I did always love
I bring thee Proof
That till I loved
I never lived – Enough –

That I shall love always –
I argue thee
That love is life –
And life hath Immortality –

This – dost thou doubt – Sweet –
Then have I
Nothing to show
But Calvary –

Emily Dickinson (1830–1886)

18 JANUARY

Of Loving at First Sight

Not caring to observe the wind,
Or the new sea explore,
Snatched from myself, how far behind
Already I behold the shore!

May not a thousand dangers sleep
In the smooth bosom of this deep?
No; 'tis so rockless and so clear,
That the rich bottom does appear,
Paved all with precious things, not torn
From shipwrecked vessels, but there born.

Sweetness, truth, and every grace
Which time and use are wont to teach,
The eye may in a moment reach,
And read distinctly in her face.

Some other nymphs, with colours faint,
And pencil slow, may Cupid paint,
And a weak heart in time destroy;
She has a stamp, and prints the boy;
Can, with a single look, inflame
The coldest breast, the rudest tame.

Edmund Waller (1606–1687)

19 JANUARY

On Stars

Stars are the nipples
of angels
pressed against the face
of heaven.

Grace Nichols (b.1950)

20 JANUARY

Mute Courtship

FROM THE PERSIAN

Love hath a language of his own,–
 A voice, that goes
From heart to heart,– whose mystic tone
 Love only knows.

The lotus-flower, whose leaves I now
 Kiss silently,
Far more than words will tell thee how
 I worship thee.

The mirror, which to thee I hold,–
 Which, when impressed
With thy bright looks, I turn and fold
 To this fond breast,–

Doth it not speak, beyond all spells
 Of poet's art,
How deep thy hidden image dwells
 In this hushed heart?

Thomas Moore (1779–1852)

21 JANUARY

The Pedlar

Lend me, a little while, the key
   That locks your heavy heart, and I'll give you back–
Rarer than books and ribbons and beads bright to see,
   This little Key of Dreams out of my pack.

The road, the road, beyond men's bolted doors,
   There shall I walk and you go free of me,
For yours lies North across the moors,
   And mine lies South. To what seas?

How if we stopped and let our solemn selves go by,
   While my gay ghost caught and kissed yours, as
     ghosts don't do,
And by the wayside, this forgotten you and I
   Sat, and were twenty-two?

Give me the key that locks your tired eyes,
   And I will lend you this one from my pack,
Brighter than coloured beads and painted books that
     make men wise:
   Take it. No, give it back!

Charlotte Mew (1869–1928)

22 JANUARY

A Dream within a Dream

Take this kiss upon the brow!
And, in parting from you now,
Thus much let me avow –
You are not wrong, who deem
That my days have been a dream;
Yet if Hope has flown away
In a night, or in a day,
In a vision, or in none,
Is it therefore the less *gone*?
All that we see or seem
Is but a dream within a dream.
I stand amid the roar
Of a surf-tormented shore,
And I hold within my hand
Grains of the golden sand –
How few! yet how they creep
Through my fingers to the deep,
While I weep – while I weep!
O God! Can I not grasp
Them with a tighter clasp?
O God! can I not save
One from the pitiless wave?
Is *all* that we see or seem
But a dream within a dream?

Edgar Allan Poe (1809–1849)

23 JANUARY

I. W. To her unconstant Lover

VERSES 1–6

As close as you your weding kept
   yet now the trueth I here:
Which you (yer now) might me have told
   what nede you nay to swere?

You know I alwayes wisht you wel
   so wyll I during lyfe:
But sith you shal a Husband be
   God sent you a good wyfe.

And this (where so you shal become)
   full boldly may you boast:
That once you had as true a Love,
   as dwelt in any Coast.

Whose constantnesse had never quaild
   if you had not begonne:
And yet it is not so far past,
   but might agayne be wonne.

If you so would: yea and not change
   so long as lyfe should last:
But yf that needes you marry must?
   then farewell hope is past.

And if you cannot be content
   to lead a single lyfe?
(Although the same right quiet be)
   then take me to your wife.

Isabella Whitney (c. 1566–1600)

24 JANUARY

'I Am Not Yours'

I am not yours, not lost in you,
   Not lost, although I long to be
Lost as a candle lit at noon,
   Lost as a snowflake in the sea.

You love me, and I find you still
   A spirit beautiful and bright,
Yet I am I, who long to be
   Lost as a light is lost in light.

Oh plunge me deep in love – put out
   My senses, leave me deaf and blind,
Swept by the tempest of your love,
   A taper in a rushing wind.

Sara Teasdale (1884–1933)

25 JANUARY

Stanzas on Woman

When lovely woman stoops to folly,
   And finds too late that men betray,
What charm can sooth her melancholy,
   What art can wash her guilt away?

The only art her guilt to cover,
   To hide her shame from every eye,
To give repentance to her lover,
   And wring his bosom – is to die.

Oliver Goldsmith (1728–1774)

26 JANUARY

i carry your heart with me(I carry it in

i carry your heart with me(i carry it in
my heart)i am never without it(anywhere
i go you go,my dear;and whatever is done
by only me is your doing,my darling)
                                i fear
no fate(for you are my fate,my sweet)i want
no world(for beautiful you are my world,my true)
and it's you are whatever a moon has always meant
and whatever a sun will always sing is you

here is the deepest secret nobody knows
(here is the root of the root and the bud of the bud
and the sky of the sky of a tree called life;which grows
higher than soul can hope or mind can hide)
and this is the wonder that's keeping the stars apart

i carry your heart(i carry it in my heart)

e.e. cummings (1894–1962)

27 JANUARY

Till all be Well

FROM *ORCHESTRA*

'When Love had shaped this world, this great fair wight,
   That all wights else in this wide womb contains,
And had instructed it to dance aright
   A thousand measures, with a thousand strains,
   Which it should practise with delightful pains,
     Until that fatal instant should revolve,
     When all to nothing should again resolve;

'The comely order and proportion fair
   On every side did please his wandering eye;
Till, glancing through the thin transparent air,
   A rude disordered rout he did espy
   Of men and women, that most spitefully
     Did one another throng and crowd so sore,
     That his kind eye, in pity, wept therefore.

'And swifter than the lightning down he came,
   Another shapeless chaos to digest;
He will begin another world to frame,
   For Love, till all be well, will never rest.
   Then with such words as cannot be expressed
     He cuts the troops, that all asunder fling,
     And ere they wist he casts them in a ring.

Sir John Davies (1569–1626)

28 JANUARY

Song

Sing in me now you words
That she may know
What love is quick in me
O come not slow

Not cold to me, but run
Molten, fiery-hot
Before Time soullessly
Make me forgot,

Or dull of image in
My dear Love's mind
You words, of power of flame
Be kind, be kind.

Ivor Gurney (1890–1937)

29 JANUARY

Song: The Scrutiny

Why should you swear I am forsworn,
   Since thine I vowed to be?
Lady, it is already morn,
   And 'twas last night I swore to thee
That fond impossibility.

Have I not loved thee much and long,
   A tedious twelve hours' space?
I must all other beauties wrong,
   And rob thee of a new embrace,
Could I still dote upon thy face.

Not but all joy in thy brown hair
   By others may be found;
But I must search the black and fair,
   Like skilful mineralists that sound
For treasure in unploughed-up ground.

Then if, when I have loved my round,
   Thou prov'st the pleasant she,
With spoils of meaner beauties crowned
   I laden will return to thee,
Even sated with variety.

Richard Lovelace (1617–1657)

30 JANUARY

Like the Touch of Rain

Like the touch of rain she was
On a man's flesh and hair and eyes
When the joy of walking thus
Has taken him by surprise:

With the love of the storm he burns,
He sings, he laughs, well I know how,
But forgets when he returns
As I shall not forget her 'Go now'.

Those two words shut a door
Between me and the blessed rain
That was never shut before
And will not open again.

Edward Thomas (1878–1917)

31 JANUARY

Ships Passing

There's a tanker on the horizon.
See the glint of the sun on its flanks;
And beyond, somewhere out there,
In all that blue-green: an oceanliner,
Too far out to be seen.
So too, the night-crossing ferry,
Observed from a distant vessel
Seems quiet from afar,
Belying the life within:
A few lights, just visible –
Specs, in the vast, rippling, dark.

And you, my love,
When will *you* return to port,
After the long voyage –
Your feet, plant, on *terra firma*?
It will be my turn to leave, then:
Duty, always calling.
How these journeys pull apart,
Where once they added to the joy
Of re-joining.

But we are weary;
Tired. Eyes strained out
To sea.
And dark is falling.

We are ships, passing.

Jana Synková (b.1968)

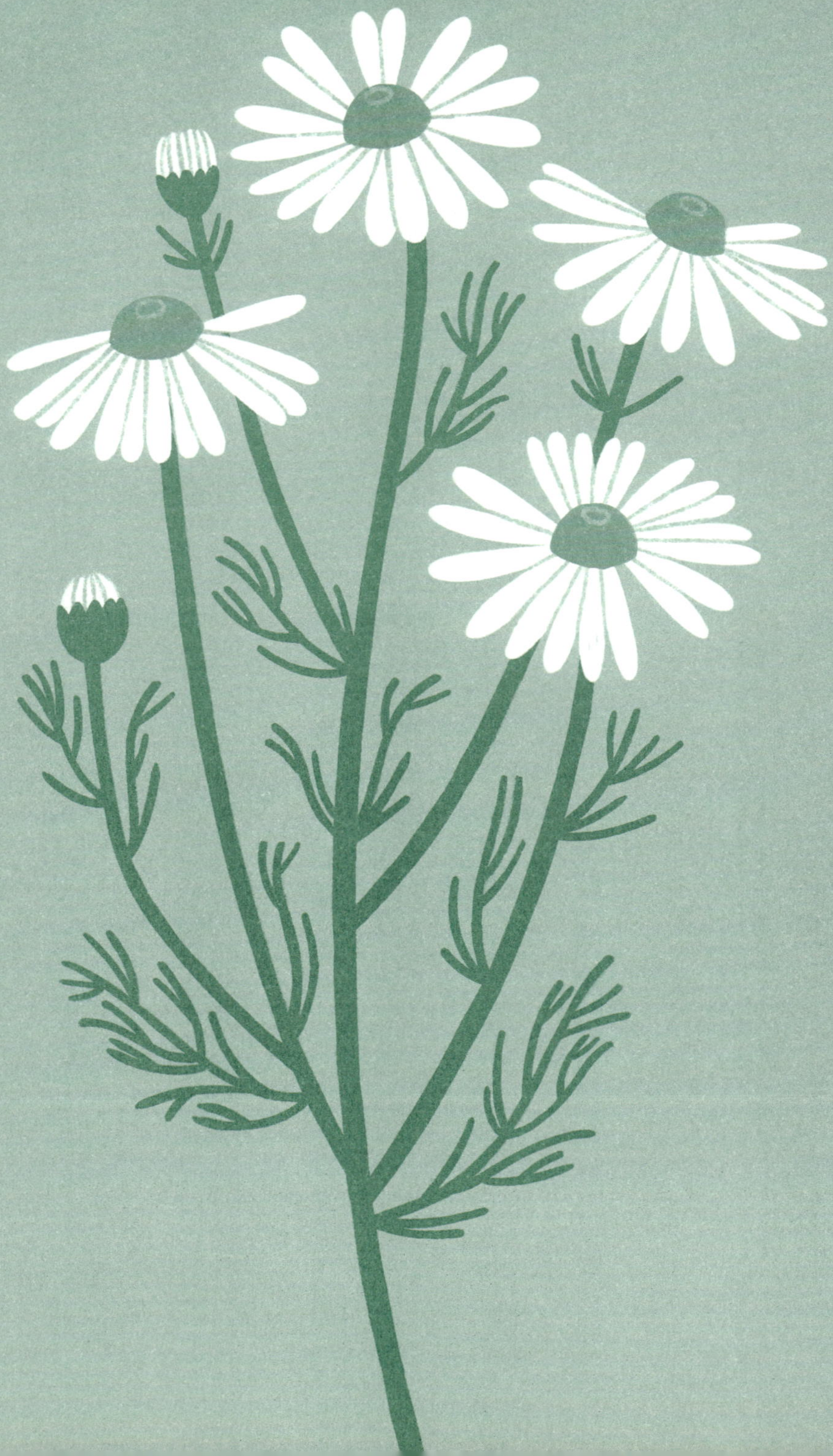

FEBRUARY

If We're Together

1 FEBRUARY

Constancy

I love her with the seasons, with the winds,
As the stars worship, as anemones
Shudder in secret for the sun, as bees
Buzz round an open flower: in all kinds
My love is perfect, and in each she finds
Herself the goal: then why, intent to tease
And rob her delicate spirit of its ease,
Hastes she to range me with inconstant minds?
If she should die, if I were left at large
On earth without her – I, on earth, the same
Quick mortal with a thousand cries, her spell
She fears would break. And I confront the charge.
As sorrowing, and as careless of my fame.
As Christ intact before the infidel.

Katherine Bradley (1846–1914) and Edith Cooper (1862–1913)
writing as
Michael Field

2 FEBRUARY

The Human Touch

'Tis the human touch in this world that counts,
   The touch of your hand and mine,
Which means far more to the fainting heart
   Than shelter and bread and wine;
For shelter is gone when the night is o'er,
   And bread lasts only a day.
But the touch of the hand and the sound of the voice
   Sing on in the soul alway.

Spencer Michael Free (1858–1938)

3 FEBRUARY

Friendship between Ephelia and Ardelia

Eph.   What *Friendship* is, ARDELIA shew.
Ard.   'Tis to love, as I love You.
Eph.   This Account, so short (tho' kind)
       Suits not my enquiring Mind.
       Therefore farther now repeat;
       What is *Friendship* when compleat?
Ard.   'Tis to share all Joy and Grief;
       'Tis to lend all due Relief
       From the Tongue, the Heart, the Hand;
       'Tis to mortgage House and Land;
       For a Friend be sold a Slave;
       'Tis to die upon a Grave,
       If a Friend therein do lie.
Eph.   This indeed, tho' carry'd high,
       This, tho' more than e'er was done
       Underneath the rolling Sun,
       This has all been said before.
       Can ARDELIA say no more?
Ard.   Words indeed no more can shew:
       But 'tis to love, as I love you.

Anne Finch (1661–1720)

4 FEBRUARY

Some Casual Passer-by

Soon we both shall share a stone
that will for ever be our own
though centuries shall pass us by:
there we, peacefully, shall lie.

And when at last we have returned to clay,
perhaps some casual passer-by will say,
'These two, once, did have their day.'
And yet, in truth, he will not know
the joy we did together know.

David Austin (1926–2018)

5 FEBRUARY

A Plaint

Dear God, 'tis hard, so awful hard to lose
The one we love, and see him go afar,
With scarce one thought of aching hearts behind,
Nor wistful eyes, nor outstretched yearning hands.
Chide not, dear God, if surging thoughts arise.
And bitter questionings of love and fate,
But rather give my weary heart thy rest,
And turn the sad, dark memories into sweet.
Dear God, I fain my loved one were anear,
But since thou will'st that happy thence he'll be,
I send him forth, and back I'll choke the grief
Rebellious rises in my lonely heart.
I pray thee, God, my loved one joy to bring;
I dare not hope that joy will be with me,
But ah, dear God, one boon I crave of thee,
That he shall ne'er forget his hours with me.

Alice Dunbar Nelson (1875–1935)

6 FEBRUARY

O Western Wind

O Western wind, when wilt thou blow
   That the small rain down can rain?
Christ, that my love were in my arms
   And I in my bed again!

Anon

7 FEBRUARY

Blest bridegroom

Blest bridegroom, this day of matrimony,
Just as you wished it, has come true;
The bride is whom you wished for . . .
                         'You
Move gracefully; your eyes are honey;
Charm was showered on your radiant face –
Yes, Aphrodite granted you outstanding praise.'

Sappho (c.630 BCE – c.570 CE)
translated by **Aaron Poochigian (b.1973)**

8 FEBRUARY

Love versus Learning

Alas, for the blight of my fancies!
   Alas, for the fall of my pride!
I planned, in my girlish romances,
   To be a philosopher's bride.

I pictured him learned and witty,
   The sage and the lover combined,
Not scorning to say I was pretty,
   Nor only adoring my mind.

No elderly, spectacled Mentor,
   But one who would worship and woo;
Perhaps I might take an inventor,
   Or even a poet would do.

And tender and gay and well-favoured,
   My fate overtook me at last:
I saw, and I heard, and I wavered,
   I smiled, and my freedom was past.

He promised to love me for ever,
   He pleaded, and what could I say?
I thought he must surely be clever,
   For he is an Oxford M.A.

But now, I begin to discover
   My visions are fatally marred;
Perfection itself as a lover,
   He's neither a sage nor a bard.

He's mastered the usual knowledge,
   And says it's a terrible bore;
He formed his opinions at college,
   Then why should he think any more?

My logic he sets at defiance,
   Declares that my Latin's no use,
And when I begin to talk Science
   He calls me a dear little goose.

He says that my lips are too rosy
   To speak in a language that's dead,
And all that is dismal and prosy
   Should fly from so sunny a head.

He scoffs at each grave occupation,
   Turns everything off with a pun;
And says that his sole calculation
   Is how to make two into one.

He says Mathematics may vary,
   Geometry cease to be true,
But scorning the slightest vagary
   He still will continue to woo.

He says that the sun may stop action,
   But he will not swerve from his course;
For love is his law of attraction,
   A smile his centripetal force.

His levity's truly terrific,
   And often I think we must part,
But compliments so scientific
   Recapture my fluttering heart.

Yet sometimes 'tis very confusing,
   This conflict of love and of lore –
But hark! I must cease from my musing,
   For that is his knock at the door!

Constance Naden (1858–1889)

9 FEBRUARY

Sonnet 140
FROM *RIME*

The lover for shamefastnesse hideth his desire
   within his faithfull hart.

The long love, that in my thought I harber,
And in my hart doth kepe his residence,
Into my face preaseth with bold pretence,
And there campeth, displaying his banner.
She that me learns to love, and to suffer,
And willes that my trust, and lustes negligence
Be reined by reason, shame, and reverence,
With his hardinesse takes displeasure.
Wherwith love to the hartes forest he fleeth,
Leaving his enterprise with paine and crye,
And there him hideth and not appeareth.
What may I do? when my maister feareth,
But in the field with him to live and dye,
For good is the life, ending faithfully.

Francesco Petraca / Petrarch (1304–1374)
translated by **Sir Thomas Wyatt (1503–1542)**

10 FEBRUARY

Sonnet 140

FROM *RIME*

Complaint of a Lover Rebuked.

Love, that liveth, and raigneth in my thought,
That built his seat within my captive brest,
Clad in the armes, wherin with me he fought,
Oft in my face he doth his banner rest.
She, that me taught to love, and suffer payne,
My doutfull hope, and eke my hote desire,
With shamefast cloke to shadowe and restraine,
Her smiling grace converteth straight to yre.
And coward love then to the hart apace
Taketh his flight, whereas he lurkes, and plaines
His purpose lost, and dare not shew his face.
For my lordes gilt thus faultlesse bide I paines.
Yet from my lorde shall not my foote remove,
Swete is his death, that takes his end by love.

Francesco Petraca / Petrarch (1304–1374)
translated by **Henry Howard, Earl of Surrey (1516/17–1547)**

11 FEBRUARY

The Shortest and Sweetest of Songs

Come
Home.

George MacDonald (1824–1905)

12 FEBRUARY

While Love is Unfashionable

for Mel

While love is unfashionable
let us live
unfashionably.
Seeing the world
a complex ball
in small hands;
love our blackest garment.
Let us be poor
in all but truth and courage
handed down
by the old
spirits.
Let us be intimate with
ancestral ghosts
and music
of the undead.

While love is dangerous
let us walk bareheaded
beside the Great River.
Let us gather blossoms
under fire.

Alice Walker (b.1944)

13 FEBRUARY

To His Coy Mistress

Had we but World enough, and Time,
This coyness Lady were no crime.
We would sit down and think which way
To walk, and pass our long Loves Day.
Thou by the *Indian Ganges* side
Should'st Rubies find: I by the Tide
Of *Humber* would complain, I would
Love you ten years before the Flood:
And you should if you please refuse
Till the Conversion of the *Jews*.
My vegetable Love should grow
Vaster than Empires, and more slow.
An hundred years should go to praise
Thine Eyes, and on thy Forehead Gaze.
Two hundred to adore each Breast:
But thirty thousand to the rest.
An Age at least to every part,
And the last Age should show your Heart.
For Lady you deserve this State;
Nor would I love at lower rate.
   But at my back I alwaies hear
Times winged Charriot hurrying near:
And yonder all before us lye
Desarts of vast Eternity.
Thy Beauty shall no more be found;
Nor, in thy marble Vault, shall sound
My ecchoing Song: then Worms shall try
That long preserv'd Virginity:
And your quaint Honour turn to dust;
And into ashes all my Lust.

The Grave's a fine and private place,
But none I think do there embrace.
   Now therefore, while the youthful hew
Sits on thy skin like morning dew,
And while thy willing Soul transpires
At every pore with instant Fires,
Now let us sport us while we may;
And now, like am'rous birds of prey,
Rather at once our Time devour,
Than languish in his slow-chapt pow'r.
Let us roll all our Strength, and all
Our sweetness, up into one Ball;
And tear our Pleasures with rough strife,
Thorough the Iron gates of Life.
Thus, though we cannot make our Sun
Stand still, yet we will make him run.

Andrew Marvell (1621–1678)

14 FEBRUARY

Seynt Valentynes Day

FROM: *THE PARLIAMENT OF FOWLS*, LINES 302-315

And in a launde, upon an hille of floures,
Was set this noble goddesse Nature;
Of braunches were hir halles and hir boures,
Y-wrought after hir craft and hir mesure;
Ne ther nas foul that cometh of engendrure,
That they ne were prest in hir presence,
To take hir doom and yeve hir audience.

For this was on seynt Valentynes day,
Whan every foul cometh ther to chese his make,
Of every kinde, that men thenke may;
And that so huge a noyse gan they make,
That erthe and see, and tree, and every lake
So ful was, that unnethe was ther space
For me to stonde, so ful was al the place.

Geoffrey Chaucer (c.1340–1400)

15 FEBRUARY

On a Romantic Lady

This poring over your *Grand Cyrus*
Must ruin you and will quite tire us.
It makes you think that an affront 'tis,
Unless your lover's an Orontes,
And courts you with a passion frantic,
In manner and in style romantic.

Now though I count myself no zero,
I don't pretend to be an hero,
Or a by-blow of him that thunders,
Nor are you one of the Seven Wonders,
But a young damsel very pretty,
And your true name is Mistress Betty.

Mary Monck (c.1678–1715)

16 FEBRUARY

To Marry or Not to Marry?
A Girl's Reverie

Mother says, 'Be in no hurry,
Marriage oft means care and worry.'

Auntie says, with manner grave,
'Wife is synonym for slave.'

Father asks, in tones commanding,
'How does Bradstreet rate his standing?'

Sister, crooning to her twins,
Sighs, 'With marriage care begins.'

Grandma, near life's closing days,
Murmurs, 'Sweet are girlhood's ways.'

Maud, twice widowed ('sod and grass')
Looks at me and moans 'Alas!'

They are six, and I am one,
Life for me has just begun.

They are older, calmer, wiser:
Age should aye be youth's adviser.

They must know – and yet, dear me,
When in Harry's eyes I see

All the world of love there burning –
On my six advisers turning,

I make answer, 'Oh, but Harry,
Is not like most men who marry.

'Fate has offered me a prize,
Life with love means Paradise.

'Life without it is not worth
All the foolish joys of earth.'

So, in spite of all they say,
I shall name the wedding-day.

Ella Wheeler Wilcox (1850–1919)

17 FEBRUARY

Love

We two that planets erst had been
Are now a double star,
And in the heavens may be seen,
Where that we fixed are.

Yet whirled with subtle power along,
Into new space we enter,
And evermore with spheral song
Revolve about one centre.

Henry David Thoreau (1817–1862)

18 FEBRUARY

Song

FROM *THE BROKEN HEART*, ACT V, SCENE III

Glories, pleasures, pomps, delights, and ease,
    Can but please
The outward senses, when the mind
Is untroubled, or by peace refin'd.
Crownes may flourish and decay,
Beauties shine, but fade away.
Youth may revell, yet it must
Lye down in a bed of dust:
Earthly honours flow and waste,
Time alone doth change and last.
Sorrows mingled with contents prepare
    Rest for care;
  Love only reigns in death; though Art
Can find no comfort for a Broken Heart.

John Ford (1586–1639)

19 FEBRUARY

Song. Love Arm'd

Love in Fantastique Triumph satt,
Whilst Bleeding Hearts around him flow'd,
For whom Fresh paines he did Create,
And strange Tyranick power he show'd;
From thy Bright Eyes he took his fire,
Which round about, in sport he hurl'd;
But 'twas from mine he took desire
Enough to undo the Amorous World.

From me he took his sighs and tears,
From thee his Pride and Crueltie;
From me his Languishments and Feares,
And every Killing Dart from thee;
Thus thou and I, the God have arm'd,
And set him up a Deity;
But my poor Heart alone is harm'd,
Whilst thine the Victor is, and free.

Aphra Behn (1640–1689)

20 FEBRUARY

To F. C.

20th FEBRUARY 1875

Fast falls the snow, O lady mine,
Sprinkling the lawn with crystals fine,
But by the gods we won't repine
   While we're together,
We'll chat and rhyme and kiss and dine,
   Defying weather.

So stir the fire and pour the wine,
And let those sea-green eyes divine
Pour their love-madness into mine:
   I don't care whether
'Tis snow or sun or rain or shine
   If we're together.

Mortimer Collins (1827–1876)

21 FEBRUARY

To Artina

I will take your <u>heart</u>.
I will take your <u>soul</u> out of your <u>body</u>
As though I were <u>God</u>.
I will not be satisfied
With the little words you say to me.
I will not be satisfied
With the touch of your hand
Nor the <u>sweet</u> of your lips <u>alone</u>.
I will take your heart for mine.
I will take your soul.
I will be God when it comes to you.

Langston Hughes (1901–1967)

22 FEBRUARY

Phillis Inamorata

Come, be my Valentine!
I'll gather eglantine,
Cowslips and sops-in-wine,
   With fragrant roses.
Down by thy Phillis sit,
She will white lilies get,
And daffadilies fit
   To make thee posies.

I have a milk-white lamb,
New-taken from the dam,
It comes where'er I am
   When I call "Willy:"
I have a wanton kid
Under my apron hid,
A colt that ne'er was rid,
   A pretty filly.

I bear in sign of love
A sparrow in my glove,
And in my breast a dove,
   This shall be all thine:
Besides of sheep a flock,
Which yieldeth many a lock,
And this shall be thy stock:
   Come, be my Valentine!

Lancelot Andrewes, Bishop of Winchester (1555–1626)

23 FEBRUARY

Laura Sleeping

Winds, whisper gently whilst she sleeps,
   And fan her with your cooling wings;
Whilst she her drops of beauty weeps
   From pure, and yet unrivall'd Springs.

Glide over Beauties Field her Face,
   To kiss her Lip, and Cheek be bold,
But with a calm, and stealing pace,
   Neither too rude; nor yet too cold.

Play in her beams, and crisp her Hair,
   With such a gale as wings soft *Love*,
And with so sweet, so rich an Air,
   As breathes from the *Arabian* Grove.

A Breath as hush't as Lovers sigh;
   Or that unfolds the Morning door;
Sweet, as the Winds, that gently fly
   To sweep the *Springs* enamell'd Floor.

Murmur soft *Musick* to her Dreams,
   That pure, and unpolluted run,
Like to the new-born Christal Streams,
   Under the bright enamour'd Sun.

But when she waking shall display
   Her light, retire within your bar,
Her Breath is life, her Eyes are day,
   And all Mankind her Creatures are.

Charles Cotton (1630–1687)

24 FEBRUARY

Wedding Morn

The morning breaks like a pomegranate
   In a shining crack of red;
Ah, when to-morrow the dawn comes late
   Whitening across the bed
It will find me watching at the marriage gate
   And waiting while light is shed
On him who is sleeping satiate
   With a sunk, unconscious head.

And when the dawn comes creeping in,
   Cautiously I shall raise
Myself to watch the daylight win
   On my first of days,
As it shows him sleeping a sleep he got
   With me, as under my gaze
He grows distinct, and I see his hot
   Face freed of the wavering blaze.

Then I shall know which image of God
   My man is made toward;
And I shall see my sleeping rod
   Or my life's reward;
And I shall count the stamp and worth
   Of the man I've accepted as mine,
Shall see an image of heaven or of earth
   On his minted metal shine.

Oh, and I long to see him sleep
   In my power utterly;
So I shall know what I have to keep. . . .
   I long to see
My love, that spinning coin, laid still
   And plain at the side of me
For me to reckon – for surely he will
   Be wealth of life to me.

And then he will be mine, he will lie
   Revealed to me;
Patent and open beneath my eye
   He will sleep of me;
He will lie negligent, resign
   His truth to me, and I
Shall watch the dawn light up for me
   This fate of mine.

And as I watch the wan light shine
   On his sleep that is filled of me,
On his brow where the curved wisps clot and twine
   Carelessly,
On his lips where the light breaths come and go
   Unconsciously,
On his limbs in sleep at last laid low
   Helplessly,
I shall weep, oh, I shall weep, I know
   For joy or for misery.

D. H. Lawrence (1885–1930)

25 FEBRUARY

Come. And Be my Baby.

The highway is full of big cars
going nowhere fast
And folks is smoking anything that'll burn
Some people wrap their lives around a cocktail glass
And you sit wondering
where you're going to turn.
I got it.
Come. And be my baby.

Some prophets say the world is gonna end tomorrow
But others say we've got a week or two
The paper is full of every kind of blooming horror
And you sit wondering
What you're gonna do.
I got it.
Come. And be my baby.

Maya Angelou (1928–2014)

26 FEBRUARY

Never seek to tell thy Love

Never seek to tell thy love
Love that never told can be;
For the gentle wind does move
Silently, invisibly.

I told my love, I told my love
I told her all my heart;
Trembling, cold, in ghastly fears,
Ah! she doth depart.

Soon as she was gone from me,
A traveller came by,
Silently, invisibly:
He took her with a sigh.

William Blake (1757–1827)

27 FEBRUARY

A Glimpse

A glimpse through an interstice caught,
Of a crowd of workmen and drivers in a bar-room around the stove late of a winter night, and I unremark'd seated in a corner,
Of a youth who loves me and whom I love, silently approaching and seating himself near, that he may hold me by the hand,
A long while amid the noises of coming and going, of drinking and oath and smutty jest,
There we two, content, happy in being together, speaking little, perhaps not a word.

Walt Whitman (1819–1892)

28 FEBRUARY

The More Loving One

Looking up at the stars, I know quite well
That, for all they care, I can go to hell,
But on earth indifference is the least
We have to dread from man or beast.

How should we like it were stars to burn
With a passion for us we could not return?
If equal affection cannot be,
Let the more loving one be me.

Admirer as I think I am
Of stars that do not give a damn,
I cannot, now I see them, say
I missed one terribly all day.

Were all stars to disappear or die,
I should learn to look at an empty sky
And feel its total dark sublime,
Though this might take me a little time.

W. H. Auden (1907–1973)

29 FEBRUARY

Prelude: Love's Immortality
FROM *THE ANGEL IN THE HOUSE*, BOOK I, CANTO VII

How vilely 'twere to misdeserve
   The poet's gift of perfect speech,
In song to try, with trembling nerve,
   The limit of its utmost reach,
Only to sound the wretched praise
   Of what to-morrow shall not be;
So mocking with immortal bays
   The cross-bones of mortality!
I do not thus. My faith is fast
   That all the loveliness I sing
Is made to bear the mortal blast,
   And blossom in a better Spring.
Doubts of eternity ne'er cross
   The Lover's mind, divinely clear:
For ever is the gain or loss
   Which maddens him with hope or fear:
So trifles serve for his relief,
   And trifles make him sick and pale;
And yet his pleasure and his grief
   Are both on a majestic scale.
The chance, indefinitely small,
   Of issue infinitely great,
Eclipses finite interests all,
   And has the dignity of fate.

Coventry Patmore (1823–1896)

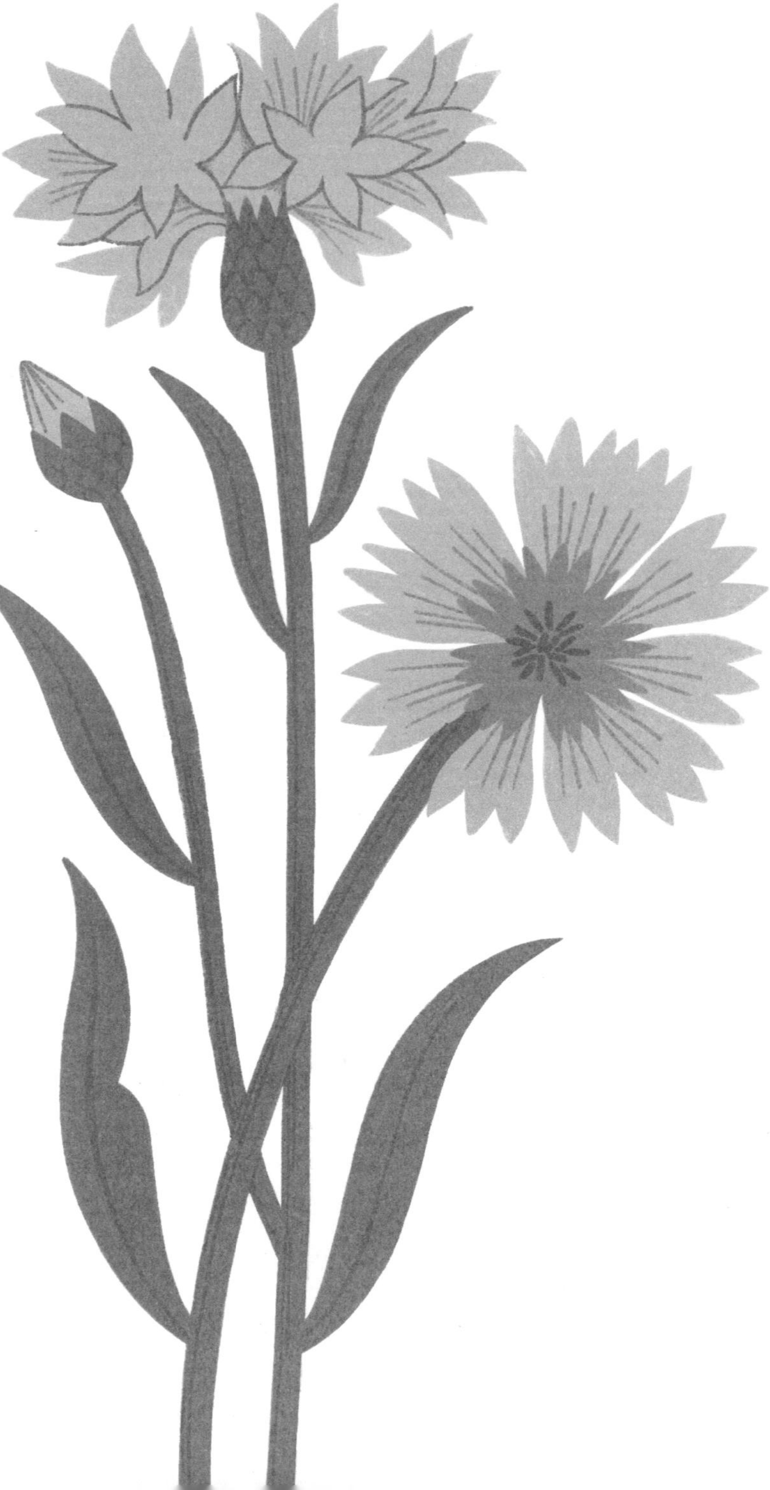

MARCH

Look in Thy Heart

1 MARCH

Sonnet 76

Why is my verse so barren of new pride,
So far from variation or quick change?
Why with the time do I not glance aside
To new-found methods and to compounds strange?
Why write I still all one, ever the same,
And keep invention in a noted weed,
That every word doth almost tell my name,
Showing their birth and where they did proceed?
O, know, sweet love, I always write of you,
And you and love are still my argument;
So all my best is dressing old words new,
Spending again what is already spent:
    For as the sun is daily new and old,
    So is my love still telling what is told.

William Shakespeare (1564–1616)

2 MARCH

no it won't be love at first sight

no
it won't
be love at
first sight when
we meet it'll be love
at first remembrance cause
i've seen you in my mother's eyes
when she tells me to marry the type
of man i'd want to raise my son to be like.

rupi kaur (b.1992)

3 MARCH

Two young men, 23 to 24 years old

He'd been in the café since ten-thirty
waiting for him to turn up soon.
Midnight came and he was waiting still.
It was nearing one-thirty; the café
had emptied almost completely.
He got tired of reading newspapers
absentmindedly. Of his paltry three shillings,
a single one was left; whilst waiting all this time,
he'd spent the rest on coffees and cognac.
He smoked all his cigarettes.
He was exhausted by such lengthy anticipation. Because.
as he was alone for hours, he began
to be seized by disturbing thoughts
about his life, which had gone astray.

But as soon as he saw his friend come in –
fatigue, boredom, and ill thoughts vanished at once.

His friend brought unexpected news.
He had won sixty pounds in a card game.

Their lovely faces, their exquisite youth,
the sensitive affection they held for each other
were refreshed, rejuvenated, invigorated
by the sixty pounds of the card game.

And full of joy and vigour, feeling and loveliness,
they went – not to the homes of their righteous families
(where anyway, they were not wanted any more):
they went to a familiar and quite particular
house of vice, they asked for a bedroom
and for expensive drinks, and drank again.

And once they'd run out of expensive drinks,
and since, by then, it was nearing four o'clock,
they abandoned themselves blissfully to love.

Constantine Cavafy (1863–1933)
translated by **Evangelos Sachperoglou (b.1941)**

4 MARCH

An Argument

To any Phillis or Chloe

I've oft been told by learned friars,
   That wishing and the crime are one,
And Heaven punishes desires
   As much as if the deed were done.

If wishing damns us, you and I
   Are damned to all our heart's content;
Come, then, at least we may enjoy
   Some pleasure for our punishment!

Thomas Moore (1779–1852)

5 MARCH

Love's Sun

Oh, can we love and live? Pray, let us die
If living cannot meet. I'll tell you why:
When dead we may both of us turn to air,
So meet in higher regions that is fair,
Thus have a calm; or, turned to waters sweet,
Posting down rivers, in the sea to meet;
Or else, our subtle motions air, mount higher,
Our heated love inflame us to one fire,
And there we're joined: one sun, your love and mine,
On mortal lovers here ever to shine.

William Cavendish, Duke of Newcastle (1592–1676)

6 MARCH

John Anderson My Jo

John Anderson my jo, John,
   When we were first acquent,
Your locks were like the raven,
   Your bonnie brow was brent;
But now your brow is beld, John,
   Your locks are like the snaw,
But blessings on your frosty pow,
   John Anderson, my jo.

John Anderson my jo, John,
   We clamb the hill thegither,
And mony a canty day, John,
   We've had wi' ane anither;
Now we maun totter down, John,
   And hand in hand we'll go,
And sleep thegither at the foot,
   John Anderson, my jo.

Robert Burns (1759–1796)

7 MARCH

Sonnet

If I were loved as I desire to be,
What is there in the great sphere of the earth,
Or range of evil between death and birth,
That I should fear, – if I were loved by thee?
All the inner, all the outer world of pain,
Clear Love would pierce and cleave, if thou wert mine,
As I have heard that somewhere in the main
Fresh-water springs come up through bitter brine.
'Twere joy, not fear, claspt hand-in-hand with thee,
To wait for death – mute – careless of all ills,
Apart upon a mountain, tho' the surge
Of some new deluge from a thousand hills
Flung leagues of roaring foam into the gorge
Below us, as far on as eye could see.

Alfred, Lord Tennyson (1809–1892)

8 MARCH

Love and Age

I played with you 'mid cowslips blowing,
When I was six and you were four;
When garlands weaving, flower-balls throwing,
Were pleasures soon to please no more.
Through groves and meads, o'er grass and heather,
With little playmates, to and fro,
We wandered hand in hand together;
But that was sixty years ago.

You grew a lovely roseate maiden,
And still our early love was strong;
Still with no care our days were laden,
They glided joyously along;
And I did love you, very dearly,
How dearly words want power to show;
I thought your heart was touched as nearly;
But that was fifty years ago.

Then other lovers came around you,
Your beauty grew from year to year,
And many a splendid circle found you
The centre of its glistening sphere.
 I saw you then, first vows forsaking,
On rank and wealth your hand bestow;
Oh, then I thought my heart was breaking, –
But that was forty years ago.

And I lived on, to wed another:
No cause she gave me to repine;
And when I heard you were a mother,
I did not wish the children mine.

My own young flock, in fair progression,
Made up a pleasant Christmas row:
My joy in them was past expression; –
But that was thirty years ago.

You grew a matron plump and comely,
You dwelt in fashion's brightest blaze;
My earthly lot was far more homely;
But I too had my festal days.
No merrier eyes have ever glistened
Around the hearth-stone's wintry glow,
Than when my youngest child was christened: –
But that was twenty years ago.

Time passed. My eldest girl was married,
And now I am a grandsire grey;
One pet of four years old I've carried
Among the wild-flowered meads to play.
In our old fields of childish pleasure,
Where now as then, the cowslips blow,
She fills her basket's ample measure, –
And that is not ten years ago.

But though love's first impassioned blindness
Has passed away in colder light,
I still have thought of you with kindness,
And shall do, till our last good-night.
The ever-rolling silent hours
Will bring a time we shall not know,
When our young days of gathering flowers
Will be a hundred years ago.

Thomas Love Peacock (1785–1866)

9 MARCH

On Earth We're Briefly Gorgeous

I

Tell me it was for the hunger
& nothing less. For hunger is to give
the body what it knows

it cannot keep. That this amber light
whittled down by another war
is all that pins my hand to your chest.

I

You, drowning
          between my arms —
stay.

You, pushing your body
          into the river
only to be left
          with yourself —
stay.

Ocean Vuong (b.1988)

10 MARCH

Loving in truth

FROM *ASTROPHIL AND STELLA*

Loving in truth, and fain in verse my love to show,
That she (dear she) might take some pleasure of my pain;
Pleasure might cause her read, reading might make her know;
Knowledge might pity win, and pity grace obtain;
    I sought fit words to paint the blackest face of woe,
Studying inventions fine her wits to entertain;
Oft turning others' leaves, to see if thence would flow
Some fresh and fruitful showers upon my sunburnt brain.
    But words came halting forth, wanting invention's stay;
Invention, nature's child, fled step-dame study's blows;
And others' feet still seemed but strangers in my way.
Thus great with child to speak and helpless in my throes,
    Biting my truant pen, beating myself for spite,
    'Fool,' said my muse to me, 'look in thy heart, and write.'

Sir Philip Sidney (1554–1586)

11 MARCH

Love Has Wings

FROM *A GIRL AT HER DEVOTIONS*

   It matters not its history; love has wings
Like lightning, swift and fatal, and it springs
Like a wild flower where it is least expected,
Existing whether cherish'd or rejected;
Living with only but to be content,
Hopeless, for love is its own element, –
Requiring nothing so that it may be
The martyr of its fond fidelity.
A mystery art thou, thou mighty one!
We speak thy name in beauty, yet we shun
To own thee, Love, a guest; the poet's songs
Are sweetest when their voice to thee belongs.

L.E.L. / Letitia Elizabeth Landen (1802–1838)

12 MARCH

Wild Nights – Wild Nights!

Wild Nights – Wild Nights!
Were I with thee
Wild Nights should be
Our luxury!

Futile – the Winds –
To a Heart in port –
Done with the Compass –
Done with the Chart!

Rowing in Eden –
Ah, the Sea!
Might I but moor – Tonight –
In Thee!

Emily Dickinson (1830–1886)

13 MARCH

Song

   Love Love to-day, my dear
   Love is not always here
Wise maids know how soon grows sere
     The greenest leaf of Spring.
       But no man knoweth
       Whither it goeth
       When the wind bloweth
        So frail a thing.

   Love Love, my dear, to-day
   If the ship's in the bay
If the bird has come your way
     That sings on summer trees.
       When his song faileth
       And the ship saileth
       No voice availeth
        To call back these.

Charlotte Mew (1869–1928)

14 MARCH

Upon the Death of Sir Albert Morton's Wife

He first deceas'd; She for a little tri'd
To live without him; lik'd it not, and di'd

Sir Henry Wotton (1538–1639)

15 MARCH

Eight O'Clock Bells

Eight o'clock bells are ringing,
Mother, may I go out?
My young man's a-waiting
For to take me out.
First he bought me apples,
Then he bought me pears,
Then he gave me sixpence
To kiss him on the stairs.

Anon

16 MARCH

Maundy Thursday

Between the brown hands of a server-lad
The silver cross was offered to be kissed.
The men came up, lugubrious, but not sad,
And knelt reluctantly, half-prejudiced.
(And kissing, kissed the emblem of a creed.)
Then mourning women knelt; meek mouths they had,
(And kissed the Body of the Christ indeed.)
Young children came, with eager lips and glad.
(These kissed a silver doll, immensely bright.)
Then I, too, knelt before that acolyte.
Above the crucifix I bent my head:
The Christ was thin, and cold, and very dead:
And yet I bowed, yea, kissed – my lips did cling.
(I kissed the warm live hand that held the thing.)

Wilfred Owen (1893–1918)

17 MARCH

Love's Good-Morrow

Pack, clouds away! and welcome day!
With night we banish sorrow;
Sweet air, blow soft, mount larks aloft
To give my love good-morrow!
Wings from the wind to please her mind,
Notes from the lark I'll borrow;
Bird, prune thy wing, nightingale, sing,
To give my love good-morrow;
To give my love good-morrow;
Notes from them both I'll borrow.

Wake from thy nest, Robin Redbreast,
Sing birds in every furrow;
And from each hill, let music shrill
Give my fair love good-morrow!
Blackbird and thrush in every bush,
Stare, linnet, and cock-sparrow!
You pretty elves, amongst yourselves,
Sing my fair love good-morrow;
To give my love good-morrow,
Sing birds in every furrow.

Thomas Heywood (1575–1641)

18 MARCH

When We Two Walked

When we two walked in Lent
We imagined that happiness
Was something different
And this was something less.

But happy were we to hide
Our happiness, not as they were
Who acted in their pride
Juno and Jupiter:

For the Gods in their jealousy
Murdered that wife and man,
And we that were wise live free
To recall our happiness then.

Edward Thomas (1878–1917)

19 MARCH

Song
FROM *TORRISMOND*, ACT I, SCENE III

How many times do I love thee, dear?
   Tell me how many thoughts there be
     In the atmosphere
       Of a new-fall'n year,
Whose white and sable hours appear
   The latest flake of Eternity:–
So many times do I love thee, dear.

How many times do I love again?
   Tell me how many beads there are
     In a silver chain
       Of evening rain,
Unravell'd from the tumbling main,
   And threading the eye of a yellow star:–
So many times do I love again.

Thomas Lovell Beddoes (1803–1849)

20 MARCH

I love you with my life

I love you with my life – 'tis so I love you;
I give you as a ring
The cycle of my days till death:
I worship with the breath
That keeps me in the world with you and spring;
And God may dwell behind, but not above you.

Mine, in the dark, before the world's beginning:
The claim of every sense,
Secret and source of every need;
The goal to which I speed,
And at my heart a vigour more immense
Than will itself to urge me to its winning.

Katherine Bradley (1846–1914) and Edith Cooper (1862–1913)
writing as
Michael Field

21 MARCH

After the Lunch

On Waterloo Bridge where we said our goodbyes,
the weather conditions bring tears to my eyes.
I wipe them away with a black woolly glove
And try not to notice I've fallen in love.

On Waterloo Bridge I am trying to think:
This is nothing, you're high on the charm and the drink.
But the juke-box inside me is playing a song
That says something different. And when was it wrong?

On Waterloo Bridge with the wind in my hair
I am tempted to skip. You're a fool. I don't care.
the head does its best but the heart is the boss –
I admit it before I am halfway across.

Wendy Cope (b.1945)

22 MARCH

Song
VERSES 1–4

Sweet are the Charms of her I love,
    More fragrant than the Damask Rose;
Soft as the Down on Turtle-Dove;
    Gentle as Air when *Zephir* blows;
Refreshing as descending Rains
To Sun-burnt Climes and thirsty Plains.

True as the Needle to the Pole
    Or as the Dial to the Sun;
Constant as gliding Waters roll,
    Whose swelling Tides obey the Moon;
From ev'ry other Charmer free,
My Life and Love shall follow thee.

The Lamb the flow'ry Thyme devours,
    The Dam the tender Kid pursues;
Sweet *Philomel* in shady Bowers
    Of verdant Spring, his Note renews:
All follow what they most admire,
As I pursue my Soul's Desire.

Nature must change her beauteous Face,
    And vary as the Seasons rise;
As Winter to the Spring gives place,
    Summer th' Approach of Autumn flies.
No Change in Love the Seasons bring,
Love only knows perpetual Spring.

Barton Booth (1682–1733)

23 MARCH

At a Dinner Party

With fruit and flowers the board is deckt,
   The wine and laughter flow;
I'll not complain – could one expect
   So dull a world to know?

You look across the fruit and flowers,
   My glance your glances find.–
It is our secret, only ours,
   Since all the world is blind.

Amy Levy (1861–1889)

24 MARCH

The Rose of Sharon
THE SONG OF SOLOMON, CHAPTER 2, VERSES 1-13

I am the rose of Sharon,
and the lily of the valleys.
As the lily among thorns,
so is my love among the daughters.
As the apple tree among the trees of the wood,
so is my beloved among the sons.
I sat down under his shadow with great delight,
and his fruit was sweet to my taste.
He brought me to the banqueting-house,
and his banner over me was love.
Stay me with flagons, comfort me with apples,
for I am sick of love.
His left hand is under my head,
and his right hand doth embrace me.
I charge you, O ye daughters of Jerusalem,
by the roes, and by the hinds of the field,
that ye stir not up, nor awake my love, till he please.
The voice of my beloved!
behold, he cometh leaping upon the mountains,
skipping upon the hills.
My beloved is like a roe or a young hart:
behold, he standeth behind our wall,
he looketh forth at the windows,
shewing himself through the lattice.
My beloved spoke, and said unto me,
'Rise up, my love, my fair one, and come away.

For, lo, the winter is past,
the rain is over and gone;
The flowers appear on the earth;
the time of the singing of birds is come,
and the voice of the turtle is heard in our land;
The fig tree putteth forth her green figs,
and the vines with the tender grape give a good smell.
Arise, my love, my fair one, and come away.'

The King James Bible

25 MARCH

The Sorrows of Werther

Werther had a love for Charlotte
   Such as words could never utter;
Would you know how first he met her?
   She was cutting bread and butter.

Charlotte was a married lady,
   And a moral man was Werther,
And, for all the wealth of Indies,
   Would do nothing for to hurt her.

So he sigh'd and pined and ogled,
   And his passion boil'd and bubbled,
Till he blew his silly brains out,
   And no more was by it troubled.

Charlotte, having seen his body
   Borne before her on a shutter,
Like a well-conducted person,
   Went on cutting bread and butter.

W. M. Thackeray (1811–1863)

26 MARCH

Love in the Age of Google

is love an abstract noun
is love a verb
is love actually on Netflix
is love a word

love is a temporary madness
love is a hurricane
love is a smoke made with the fume of sighs
love is a losing game

can love last forever
can love break your heart
can love2shop vouchers be used online
can lovebites scar

love can build a bridge
love can set you free
love can hurt ed sheeran
love cannot heal me

does love cure depression
does love have an age
does lovejoy marry charlotte
does love always fade

love does not need an explanation
love does not exist
love doesn't need a slogan
love is all there is

Brian Bilston / Paul Millicheap (b.1970)

27 MARCH

If

If life were but a dream, my Love,
  And death the waking time;
If day had not a beam, my Love,
  And night had not a rhyme, –
    A barren, barren world were this
    Without one saving gleam;
    I'd only ask that with a kiss
    You'd wake me from the dream.

If dreaming were the sum of days,
  And loving were the bane;
If battling for a wreath of bays
  Could soothe a heart in pain, –
    I'd scorn the meed of battle's might,
    All other aims above
    I'd choose the human's higher right,
    To suffer and to love!

Paul Laurence Dunbar (1872–1906)

28 MARCH

Annabel Lee

It was many and many a year ago,
   In a kingdom by the sea,
That a maiden there lived whom you may know
   By the name of Annabel Lee;
And this maiden she lived with no other thought
   Than to love and be loved by me.

I was a child and *she* was a child,
   In this kingdom by the sea,
But we loved with a love that was more than love –
   I and my Annabel Lee –
With a love that the wingèd seraphs of Heaven
   Coveted her and me.

And this was the reason that, long ago,
   In this kingdom by the sea,
A wind blew out of a cloud, chilling
   My beautiful Annabel Lee;
So that her highborn kinsmen came
   And bore her away from me,
To shut her up in a sepulchre
   In this kingdom by the sea.

The angels, not half so happy in Heaven,
   Went envying her and me–
Yes!–that was the reason (as all men know,
   In this kingdom by the sea)
That the wind came out of the cloud by night,
   Chilling and killing my Annabel Lee.

But our love it was stronger by far than the love
   Of those who were older than we –
   Of many far wiser than we –
And neither the angels in Heaven above
   Nor the demons down under the sea
Can ever dissever my soul from the soul
   Of the beautiful Annabel Lee;

For the moon never beams, without bringing me dreams
   Of the beautiful Annabel Lee;
And the stars never rise, but I feel the bright eyes
   Of the beautiful Annabel Lee;
And so, all the night-tide, I lie down by the side
   Of my darling – my darling – my life and my bride,
   In her sepulchre there by the sea –
   In her tomb by the sounding sea.

Edgar Allan Poe (1809–1849)

29 MARCH

Evening Song

Dear love, what thing of all the things that be
Is ever worth one thought from you or me,
      Save only Love,
      Save only Love?

The days so short, the nights so quick to flee,
The world so wide, so deep and dark the sea,
      So dark the sea;

So far the suns and every listless star,
Beyond their light – Ah! dear, who knows how far,
      Who knows how far?

One thing of all dim things I know is true,
The heart within me knows, and tells it you,
      And tells it you.

So blind is life, so long at last is sleep,
And none but Love to bid us laugh or weep,
      And none but Love,
      And none but Love.

Willa Cather (1873–1947)

30 MARCH

Song to a Fair Young Lady
GOING OUT OF THE TOWN IN THE SPRING

Ask not the Cause why sullen *Spring*
   So long delays her Flow'rs to bear;
Why warbling Birds forget to sing,
   And Winter Storms invert the Year?
Chloris is gone; and Fate provides
To make it *Spring*, where she resides.

Chloris is gone, the Cruel Fair;
   She cast not back a pitying Eye:
But left her Lover in Despair,
   To sigh, to languish, and to die:
Ah, how can those fair Eyes endure
To give the Wounds they will not cure!

Great God of Love, why hast thou made
   A Face that can all Hearts command,
That all Religions can invade,
   And change the Laws of ev'ry Land?
Where thou hadst plac'd such Pow'r before,
Thou shou'dst have made her Mercy more.

When *Chloris* to the Temple comes,
   Adoring Crowds before her fall;
She can restore the Dead from Tombs,
   And ev'ry Life but mine recall.
I only am by Love design'd
To be the Victim for Mankind.

John Dryden (1631–1700)

31 MARCH

Rondeau

Jenny kissed me when we met,
    Jumping from the chair she sat in;
Time, you thief, who love to get
    Sweets into your list, put that in:
Say I'm weary, say I'm sad,
    Say that health and wealth have missed me,
Say I'm growing old, but add,
    Jenny kissed me.

Leigh Hunt (1784–1859)

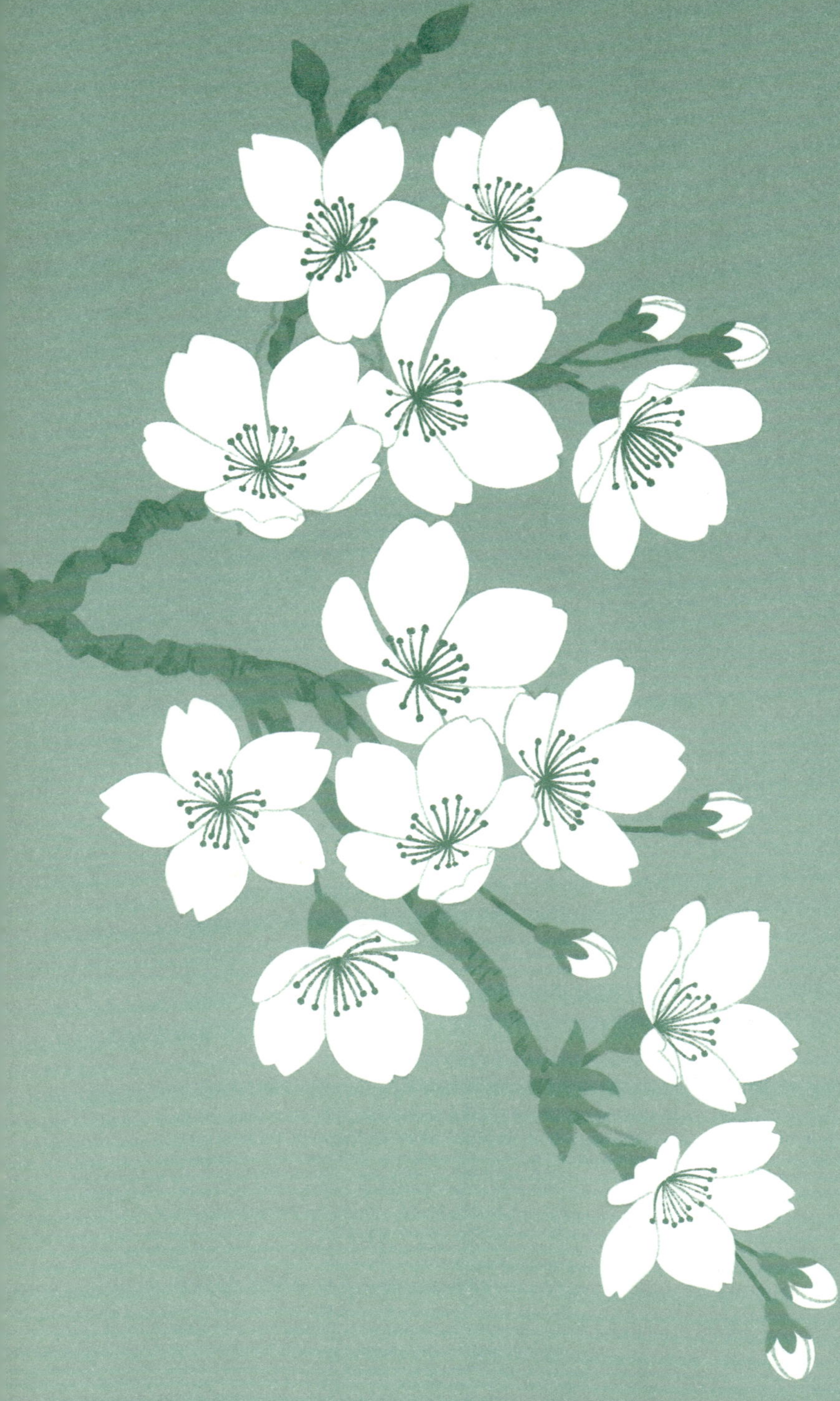

APRIL

What Joys Exceeding

1 APRIL

The Lady's Mistake

    That his eyebrows were false – that his hair
      Was assumed, I was fully aware!
I knew his moustache of a barber was bought
And that Cartwright provided his teeth – but I thought
      That his *heart* was, at least, true and fair

    I saw that the exquisite glow
      Spreading over the cheek of my beau
From a carmine shell came and I often was told
That his elegant calf by his tailor was sold
      I dreamed not his *love* was but show

    I was sure – I could easily tell
      That the form which deluded each belle
Was made over his own – but I could not believe
That his flattering tongue, too, was taught to deceive
      That his *fortune* was humbug, as well

    I had made up my mind to dispense
      With a figure, hair, teeth, heart & sense
The calf I'd o'erlook were it ever so small
But to think that he is not a *count* after all
      That's a not to be pardoned offence!

Frances Sargent Osgood (1811–1850)

2 APRIL

Some Call it Love

I am a flower
you can put me
in your window

I don't need seed soil
only a bit of water
some sunshine
every now and then
and a kiss

I may not grow
but I'll stick
around

and wave to you
each morning

Nikki Giovanni (b.1943)

3 APRIL

Sonnet LXX

FROM *AMORETTI*

Fresh spring the herald of loves mighty king,
    In whose cote armour richly are displayed
    all sorts of flowers the which on earth do spring
  in goodly colours gloriously arrayd.
Goe to my love, where she is carelesse layd,
  yet in her winters bowre not well awake:
  tell her the joyous time wil not be staid
  unless she doe him by the forelock take.
Bid her therefore her selfe soone ready make,
  to wayt on love amongst his lovely crew:
  where every one that misseth then her make,
  shall be by him amearst with penance dew.
Make hast therefore sweet love, whilest it is prime,
  for none can call againe the passed time.

Edmund Spenser (c.1552–1599)

4 APRIL

XXI

FROM *SONNETS FROM THE PORTUGUESE*

Say over again, and yet once over again,
That thou dost love me. Though the word repeated
Should seem 'a cuckoo-song,' as thou dost treat it,
Remember, never to the hill or plain,
Valley and wood, without her cuckoo-strain
Comes the fresh Spring in all her green completed.
Belovèd, I, amid the darkness greeted
By a doubtful spirit-voice, in that doubt's pain
Cry, . . . 'Speak once more – thou lovest!' Who can fear
Too many stars, though each in heaven shall roll,
Too many flowers, though each shall crown the year?
Say thou dost love me, love me, love me – toll
The silver iterance! – only minding, Dear,
To love me also in silence with thy soul.

Elizabeth Barrett Browning (1806–1861)

5 APRIL

The Constant Lover

Out upon it, I have loved
   Three whole days together;
And am like to love three more,
   If it prove fair weather.

Time shall moult away his wings
   Ere he shall discover
In such whole wide world again
   Such a constant lover.

But the spite on't is, no praise
   Is due at all to me:
Love with me had made no stays
   Had it any been but she,

Had it any been but she,
   And that very face,
There had been at least ere this
   A dozen dozen in her place.

Sir John Suckling (1609–1642)

6 APRIL

Camomile Tea

Outside the sky is light with stars;
There's a hollow roaring from the sea.
And, alas! for the little almond flowers,
The wind is shaking the almond tree.

How little I thought, a year ago,
In the horrible cottage upon the Lee
That he and I should be sitting so
And sipping a cup of camomile tea!

Light as feathers the witches fly,
The horn of the moon is plain to see;
By a firefly under a jonquil flower
A goblin toasts a bumble-bee.

We might be fifty, we might be five,
So snug, so compact, so wise are we!
Under the kitchen-table leg
My knee is pressing against his knee.

Our shutters are shut, the fire is low,
The tap is dripping peacefully;
The saucepan shadows on the wall
Are black and round and plain to see.

Katherine Mansfield (1888–1923)

7 APRIL

Cloe to Aminta.
On the Loss of her Lover

        Cloe.
Tell – dear Aminta, now 'tis over,
How came you to lose your Lover|
        Aminta.
Tell me, first, how I obtained him.
        Cloe.
O, 'twas Youth and Beauty gain'd him.
        Aminta.
My Youth and Beauty *still* remain;
Yet, you see, I have lost the Swain.
Ah! my Girl, the Thing's too certain;
Th' Pangs he felt, were for my Fortune.
Why – five and forty – thousand – Pound!
Had given the Great *Mogul* a wound!
The Mighty *Czar*, had He been living,
Had thought the Present worth receiving.
But – that delightful *South-Sea* Scheme;
That charming, warming, *golden* Dream,
Which made so many Fools and Knaves
And left so many well-bred *Slaves*;
Fell to the Depths from whence it came,
And quench'd at *once* his tow'ring flame.

Sarah Dixon (1672–1765)

8 april

The Cherry Trees

Out of the dusk of distant woods
All round the April skies
Blossom-white, the cherry trees
Like lovely apparitions rise,

Like spirits strange to this ill world,
White strangers from a world apart,
Like silent promises of peace,
Like hope that blossoms in the heart.

Laurence Binyon (1869–1943)

9 APRIL

Before They Are Changed by Time

They were so very sad during their separation.
It was not what they wanted; it was circumstances.
Necessities of life forced one of them to leave
and travel far away – New York or Canada.
Their love for sure was not what it once used to be;
the sexual attraction had gradually waned,
the sexual attraction had been reduced a lot.
Yet to be separated was not what they wanted.
It was circumstances. – Or maybe Destiny
appeared like an artist separating them now,
before their feeling fades, before they are changed by Time;
each of them for the other will then remain forever
a twenty-four-year-old and beautiful young man.

Constantine Cavafy (1863–1993)
translated by **Evangelos Sachperoglou (b.1941)**

10 APRIL

The Good Morrow

I wonder by my troth, what thou, and I
Did, till we lov'd? were we not wean'd till then?
But suck'd on countrey pleasures, childishly?
Or snorted we in the seaven sleepers den?
T'was so; But this, all pleasures fancies bee
If ever any beauty did I see,
Which I desir'd, and got, t'was but a dreame of thee.

And now good morrow to our waking soules,
Which watch not one another out of feare;
For love, all love of other sights controules,
And makes one little room, an every where.
Let sea-discoverers to new worlds have gone,
Let Maps to other, worlds on worlds have showne,
Let us possesse one world, each hath one, and is one.

My face in thine eye, thine in mine appeares,
And true plaine hearts doe in the faces rest,
Where can we finde two better hemispheares
Without sharpe North, without declining West?
What ever dyes, was not mixt equally;
If our two loves be one, or, thou and I
Love so alike, that none doe slacken, none can die.

John Donne (1572–1631)

11 APRIL

Sonnet

Eyes, calm beside thee, (Lady, could'st thou know!)
   May turn away thick with fast-gathering tears:
I glance not where all gaze: thrilling and low
   Their passionate praises reach thee – my cheek wears
Alone no wonder when thou passest by;
Thy tremulous lids bent and suffused reply
To the irrepressible homage which doth glow
   On every lip but mine: if in thine ears
Their accents linger – and thou dost recall
   Me as I stood, still, guarded, very pale,
Beside each votarist whose lighted brow
Wore worship like an aureole, 'O'er them all
   My beauty,' thou wilt murmur, 'did prevail
Save that one only, – Lady, could'st thou know!

Robert Browning (1812–1889)

12 APRIL

A Joke Versified

'Come, come,' said Tom's father, 'at your time of life,
   'There's no longer excuse for thus playing the rake –
'It is time you should think, boy, of taking a wife.'–
   'Why, so it is, father – whose wife shall I take?'

Thomas Moore (1779–1852)

13 APRIL

Charita

FROM *THE COUNTESS OF PEMBROKE'S ARCADIA*

My true love hath my hart, and I have his,
By just exchange, one for the other giv'ne.
I holde his deare, and myne he cannot misse:
There never was a better bargain driv'ne.

His hart in me, keepes me and him in one,
My hart in him, his thoughtes and senses guides:
He loves my hart, for once it was his owne:
I cherish his, because in me it bides.

His hart his wound receaved from my sight:
My hart was wounded, with his wounded hart,
For as from me, on him his hurt did light,
So still me thought in me his hurt did smart:
    Both equall hurt, in this change sought our blisse:
    My true love hath my hart and I have his.

Sir Philip Sidney (1554–1586)

14 APRIL

Conviction (IV)

I like to get off with people,
I like to lie in their arms,
I like to be held and tightly kissed,
Safe from all alarms.

I like to laugh and be happy
With a beautiful beautiful kiss,
I tell you, in all the world
There is no bliss like this.

Stevie Smith (1902–1971)

15 APRIL

The Definition of Love

i
My Love is of a birth as rare
As 'tis for object strange and high;
It was begotten by despair
Upon Impossibility.

ii
Magnanimous Despair alone
Could show me so divine a thing
Where feeble Hope could ne'er have flown,
But vainly flapt its Tinsel Wing.

iii
And yet I quickly might arrive
Where my extended Soul is fixt,
But Fate does Iron wedges drive,
And alwais crouds it self betwixt.

iv
For Fate with jealous Eye does see
Two perfect Loves, nor lets them close;
Their union would her ruine be,
And her Tyrannick pow'r depose.

v

And therefore her Decrees of Steel
Us as the distant Poles have plac'd,
(Though Love's whole World on us doth wheel)
Not by themselves to be embrac'd;

vi

Unless the giddy Heaven fall,
And Earth some new Convulsion tear;
And, us to joyn, the World should all
Be cramp'd into a *Planisphere*.

vii

As Lines, so Loves *oblique* may well
Themselves in every Angle greet;
But ours so truly *Paralel*,
Though infinite, can never meet.

viii

Therefore the Love which us doth bind,
But Fate so enviously debars,
Is the Conjunction of the Mind,
And Opposition of the Stars.

Andrew Marvell (1621–1678)

16 APRIL

The Visitor

She brings that breath, and music too,
That comes when April's days begin;
And sweetness Autumn never had
In any bursting skin.

She's big with laughter at the breasts
Like netted fish they leap:
Oh God, that I were far from here,
Or lying fast asleep!

W. H. Davies (1871–1940)

17 APRIL

She dwelt among the untrodden ways

She dwelt among the untrodden ways
   Beside the springs of Dove,
A Maid whom there were none to praise
   And very few to love:

A violet by a mossy stone
   Half hidden from the eye!
– Fair as a star, when only one
   Is shining in the sky.

She lived unknown, and few could know
   When Lucy ceased to be;
But she is in her grave, and, oh,
   The difference to me!

William Wordsworth (1770–1850)

18 APRIL

Are You the New Person Drawn toward Me?

Are you the new person drawn toward me?
To begin with, take warning, I am surely far different from what you suppose;
Do you suppose you will find in me your ideal?
Do you think it so easy to have me become your lover?
Do you think the friendship of me would be unalloy'd satisfaction?
Do you think I am trusty and faithful?
Do you see no further than this façade, this smooth and tolerant manner of me?
Do you suppose yourself advancing on real ground toward a real heroic man?
Have you no thought, O dreamer, that it may be all maya, illusion?

Walt Whitman (1819–1892)

19 APRIL

When Did It Happen?

When did it happen?
    'It was a long time ago.'

Where did it happen?
    'It was far away.'

No, tell. Where did it happen?
    'In my heart.'

What is your heart doing now?
    'Remembering. Remembering.'

Mary Oliver (1935–2019)

20 APRIL

O what unhop't for sweet supply!

O what unhop't for sweet supply!
   O what joyes exceeding!
What an affecting charme feele I,
   From delight proceeding!
That which I long despair'd to be,
   To her I am, and shee to mee.

Shee that alone in cloudy griefe
   Long to mee appeared,
Shee now alone with bright reliefe
   All those clouds hath cleared.
Both are immortall and divine,
   Since I am hers, and she is mine.

Thomas Campion (1567–1620)

21 APRIL

To My Dear and Loving Husband

If ever two were one, then surely we.
If ever man were lov'd by wife, then thee;
If ever wife was happy in a man,
Compare with me ye women, if you can.
I prize thy love more than whole Mines of gold,
Or all the riches that the East doth hold.
My love is such that Rivers cannot quench,
Nor ought but love from thee give recompense.
Thy love is such I can no way repay,
The heavens reward thee manifold, I pray.
Then while we live, in love lets so persever,
That when we live no more, we may live ever.

Anne Bradstreet (c.1612–1672)

22 APRIL

Measurements

Our world is very little in the sky,
   Far off she must be just a mote to see;
   And on the tiny ball creep tinier we,
To live a very little while, and die.

My love is very great within my heart;
   It sees in two dear eyes, infinity,
   It finds in one sweet hour, eternity,
It has one measure: – nearness, or apart.

Ah, well! both things are true as truth can be!
   The world is little and my love is great;
   Yet who would rise triumphant over fate
Earth's breadth, love's narrowness, must learn to see.

L. S. Bevington (1845–1895)

23 APRIL

It was a lover and his lass
FROM *AS YOU LIKE IT*, ACT V, SCENE III

It was a lover and his lass,
   With a hey, and a ho, and a hey-nonny-no,
That o'er the green cornfield did pass,
   In spring-time, the only pretty ring-time,
When birds do sing, hey ding-a-ding ding,
Sweet lovers love the spring.

Between the acres of the rye,
   With a hey, and a ho, and a hey-nonny-no,
Those pretty country folks would lie,
   In spring-time, the only pretty ring-time,
When birds do sing, hey ding-a-ding ding,
Sweet lovers love the spring.

This carol they began that hour,
   With a hey, and a ho, and a hey-nonny-no,
How that a life was but a flower
   In spring-time, the only pretty ring-time,
When birds do sing, hey ding-a-ding ding,
Sweet lovers love the spring.

And therefore take the present time,
   With a hey, and a ho, and a hey-nonny-no,
For love is crownèd with the prime
   In spring-time, the only pretty ring-time,
When birds do sing, hey ding-a-ding ding,
Sweet lovers love the spring.

William Shakespeare (1564–1616)

24 APRIL

Time Now Makes A New Beginning

FROM *BIRTH BELLS FOR LOUISA*

Time now makes a new beginning.
The world is both outside and inside.
    Live with our love.

At this moment there is no past
And consciousness is everywhere.
    Live with our love.

The world is both outside and inside
And now the worlds must be united.
    Live with our love.

And consciousness is everywhere
Of newly integrated spaces.
    Live with our love.

And now the worlds must be united
Into a manifold of being.
    Live with our love.

Of newly integrated spaces
What shall we say except that they
    Live with our love?

Into a manifold of being
Time now makes its new beginning.
    Live with our love, with our love.

John Fuller (b.1937)

25 APRIL

Strephon to Celia. A Modern Love-Letter

Madam

   I hope you'll think it's true
I deeply am in Love with you,
When I assure you t'other Day,
As I was musing on my way,
At thought of you I tumbled down
Directly in a deadly Swoon:
And though 'tis true I'm something better,
Yet I can hardly spell my Letter:
And as the latter you may view,
I hope you'll think the former true.
You need not wonder at my Flame,
For you are not a mortal Dame:
I saw you dropping from the Skies;
And let dull Idiots swear your Eyes
With Love their glowing Breast inspire,
I tell you they are Flames of Fire,
That scorch my Forehead to a Cinder,
And burn my very Heart to a Tinder.
Your Breast so mighty cold, I trow,
Is made of nothing else but Snow:
Your Hands (no wonder they have Charms)
Are made of Iv'ry like your Arms.
Your Cheeks, that look as if they bled,
Are nothing else but Roses red.
Your Lips are Coral very bright,
Your Teeth – tho' Numbers out of spite
May say they're Bones – yet 'twill appear
They're Rows of Pearls exceeding dear.

Now, Madam, as the Chat goes round,
I hear you have ten thousand Pound:
But that as I a Trifle hold,
Give me your Person, dem your Gold;
Yet for your own Sake 'tis secured,
I hope– your Houses too ensur'd;
I'd have you take a special Care,
And of false Mortgages beware;
You've Wealth enough 'tis true, but yet
You want a Friend to manage it.
Now such a Friend you soon might have,
By fixing on your humble Slave;
Not that I mind a stately House,
Or value Mony of a Louse;
But your Five hundred Pounds a Year,
I wou'd secure it for my Dear:
Then smile upon your Slave, that lies
Half-murder'd by your radiant Eyes;
Or else this very Moment dies –
                Strephon

Mary Leapor (1722–1746)

26 APRIL

Caelica

Love, the delight of all well-thinking minds,
　Delight, the fruit of virtue dearly loved,
Virtue, the highest good, that reason finds,
　Reason, the fire wherein men's thoughts be proved,
Are from the world by Nature's power bereft,
And in one creature, for her glory, left.

Beauty, her cover is, the eye's true pleasure;
　In honour's fame she lives; the ear's sweet music;
Excess of wonder grows from her true measure;
　Her worth is passion's wound, and passion's physic;
From her true heart, clear springs of wisdom flow,
Which, imaged in her words and deeds, men know.

Time fain would stay, that she might never leave her,
　Place doth rejoice, that she must needs contain her,
Death craves of heaven, that she may not bereave her,
　The heavens know their own, and do maintain her.
Delight, Love, Reason, Virtue, let it be,
To set all women light, but only she.

Fulke Greville, Lord Brooke (1554–1628)

27 APRIL

Sonnet

Oh! Death will find me, long before I tire
   Of watching you; and swing me suddenly
Into the shade and loneliness and mire
   Of the last land! There, waiting patiently,

One day, I think, I'll feel a cool wind blowing,
   See a slow light across the Stygian tide,
And hear the Dead about me stir, unknowing,
   And tremble. And *I* shall know that you have died,

And watch you, a broad-browed and smiling dream,
   Pass, light as ever, through the lightless host,
Quietly ponder, start, and sway, and gleam –
   Most individual and bewildering ghost! –

And turn, and toss your brown delightful head
Amusedly, among the ancient Dead.

April 1909.

Rupert Brooke (1887–1915)

28 APRIL

Hinterhof

Stay near to me and I'll stay near to you –
As near as you are dear to me will do,
   Near as the rainbow to the rain,
   The west wind to the windowpane,
As fire to the hearth, as dawn to dew.

Stay true to me and I'll stay true to you –
As true as you are new to me will do,
   New as the rainbow in the spray,
   Utterly new in every way,
New in the way that what you say is true.

Stay near to me, stay true to me. I'll stay
As near, as true to you as heart could pray.
   Heart never hoped that one might be
   Half of the things you are to me –
The dawn, the fire, the rainbow and the day.

James Fenton (b.1949)

29 APRIL

Sampler Verse (1818)

Ann thou art divinely fair
Nor can I in this work declare
Near half the beauties of thine

Anon

30 APRIL

She Walks in Beauty

I

She walks in beauty, like the night
Of cloudless climes and starry skies;
And all that's best of dark and bright
Meet in her aspect and her eyes;
Thus mellowed to that tender light
Which heaven to gaudy day denies.

II

One shade the more, one ray the less,
Had half impair'd the nameless grace
Which waves in every raven tress,
Or softly lightens o'er her face;
Where thoughts serenely sweet express,
How pure, how dear their dwelling-place.

III

And on that cheek, and o'er that brow,
So soft, so calm, yet eloquent,
The smiles that win, the tints that glow,
But tell of days in goodness spent,
A mind at peace with all below,
A heart whose love is innocent!

Lord George Gordon Byron (1788–1824)

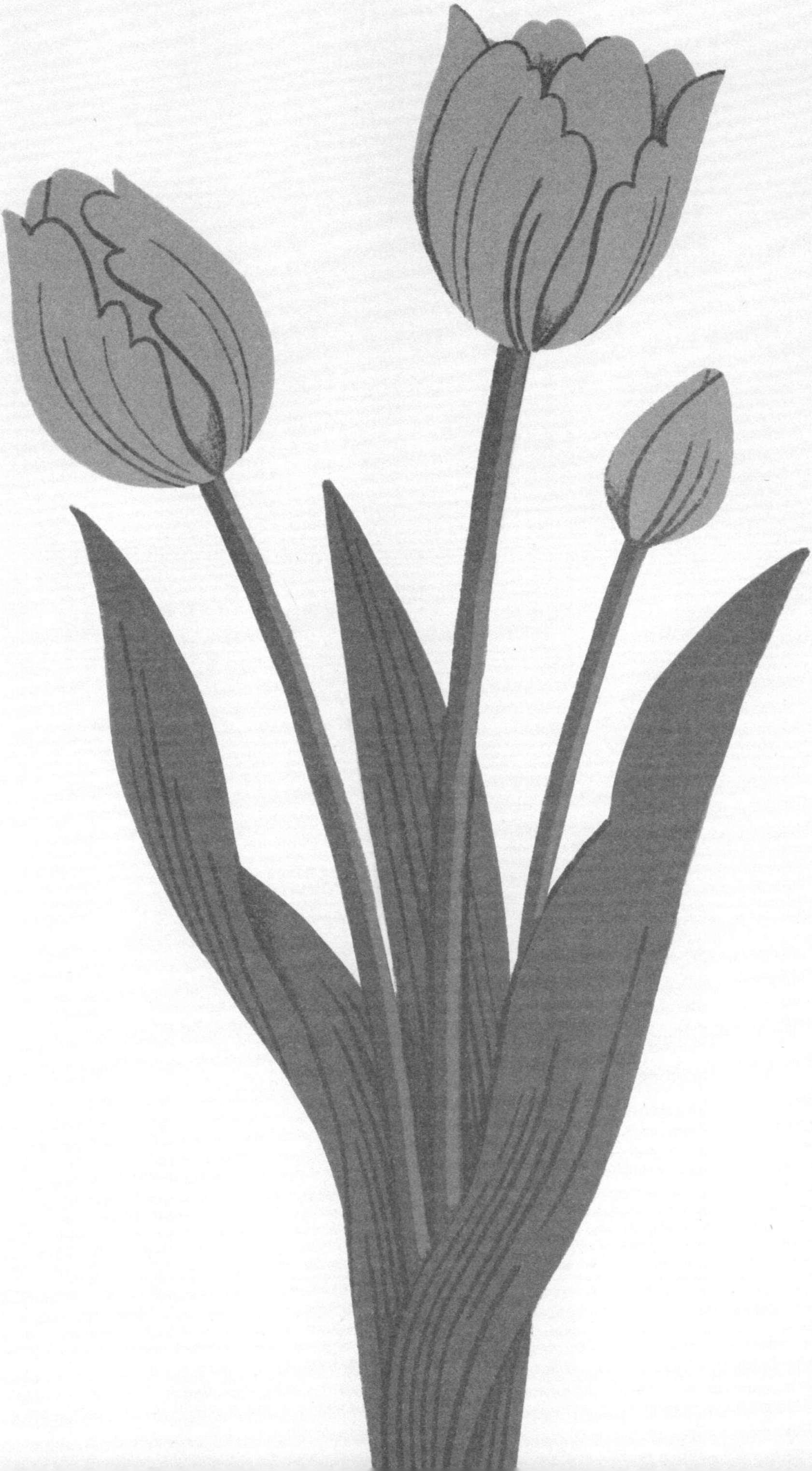

MAY

Trust All to Love

1 MAY

Sonnet 29

When, in disgrace with fortune and men's eyes,
I all alone beweep my outcast state,
And trouble deaf heaven with my bootless cries,
And look upon myself and curse my fate,
Wishing me like to one more rich in hope,
Featured like him, like him with friends possessed,
Desiring this man's art and that man's scope,
With what I most enjoy contented least;
Yet in these thoughts myself almost despising,
Haply I think on thee, and then my state,
Like to the lark at break of day arising
From sullen earth, sings hymns at heaven's gate;
    For thy sweet love remembered such wealth brings
    That then I scorn to change my state with kings.

William Shakespeare (1564–1616)

2 MAY

The Sun has Burst the Sky

The sun has burst the sky
Because I love you
And the river its banks.

The sea laps the great rocks
Because I love you
And takes no heed of the moon dragging it away
And saying coldly 'Constancy is not for you'.

The blackbird fills the air
Because I love you
With spring and lawns and shadows falling on lawns.

The people walk in the street and laugh
I love you
And far down the river ships sound their hooters
Crazy with joy because I love you.

Jenny Joseph (b.1932)

3 MAY

With thee conversing

FROM *PARADISE LOST*, BOOK IV, LINES 639-652

With thee conversing I forget all time,
All seasons, and their change, all please alike.
Sweet is the breath of morn, her rising sweet,
With charm of earliest birds; pleasant the sun,
When first on this delightful land he spreads
His orient beams, on herb, tree, fruit, and flower,
Glistering with dew; fragrant the fertile earth
After soft showers; and sweet the coming-on
Of grateful evening mild; then silent night
With this her solemn bird and this fair moon,
And these the gems of heaven, her starry train:
But neither breath of morn, when she ascends
With charm of earliest birds, nor rising sun
On this delightful land, nor herb, fruit, flower,
Glistering with dew, nor fragrance after showers;
Nor grateful evening mild, nor silent night
With this her solemn bird, nor walk by moon,
Or glittering starlight without thee is sweet

John Milton (1608–1674)

4 MAY

Lightness

It was your lightness that drew me,
the lightness of your talk and your laughter,
the lightness of your cheek in my hands,
your sweet gentle modest lightness;
and it is the lightness of your kiss
that is starving my mouth,
and the lightness of your embrace
that will let me go adrift.

Meg Bateman (b.1959)
translated from the Gaelic by the author

5 MAY

White and Blue

My love is of comely height and straight,
And comely in all her ways and gait,
She shows in her face the rose's hue,
And her lids on her eyes are white on blue.

When Elemley club-men walk'd in May,
And folk came in clusters every way,
As soon as the sun dried up the dew,
And clouds in the sky were white on blue,

She came by the down with tripping walk,
By daisies and shining banks of chalk,
And brooks with the crowfoot flow'rs to strew
The sky-tinted water, white on blue;

She nodded her head as play'd the band,
She tapp'd with her foot as she did stand,
She danc'd in a reel, and wore all new
A skirt with a jacket, white with blue.

I singled her out from thin and stout,
From slender and stout I chose her out,
And what in the evening could I do
But give her my breast-knot, white and blue?

William Barnes (1801–1886)

6 MAY

Gardener's Grief

VERSES 1–3

I'm a broken-hearted Gardener, and don't know what to do,
My love she is inconstant, and a fickle jade, too,
One smile from her lips will never be forgot,
It refreshes, like a shower from a watering pot.

CHORUS: *Oh, Oh! she's a fickle wild rose,*
A damask, a cabbage, a young China Rose.

She's my myrtle, my geranium,
My Sun flower, my sweet marjorum,
My honey suckle, my tulip, my violet,
My holy hock, my dahlia, my mignonette.

We grew up together like two apple trees,
And clung to each other like double sweet peas,
Now they're going to trim her, and plant her in a pot,
And I'm left to wither, neglected and forgot.

Victorian Street Ballad

7 MAY

A New Courtly Sonet, of the Lady Greensleeves

TO THE NEW TUNE OF GREENSLEEVES, 1584
VERSE 1

Alas my love ye do me wrong
   To cast me off discourteously:
And I have loved you so long
   Delighting in your companie.

Greensleeves was all my joy,
   Greensleeves was my delight:
Greensleeves was my heart of of gold, –
   And who but my ladie Greensleeves

Anon

8 MAY

The Errand

Arise, my trusty page
    Saddle your horse, then spring
Upon his back and speed away
    To the palace of the king.
There seek some stable boy or groom
    And ask of him, 'I pray,
Tell me which daughter of the king
    Becomes a bride today?'

And if he says, 'The dark-haired one,'
    Bring me the news with speed,
But if he says, 'The light-haired one,'
    You need not urge your steed.
But leisurely retrace your way
    In silence, till you see
The rope-walk. Buy a good stout cord
    And fetch it home to me.

Heinrich Heine (1797–1856)
translated by **Willa Cather (1873–1947)**

9 MAY

Against Constancy

Tell me no more of constancy,
   That frivolous pretence
Of cold age, narrow jealousy,
   Disease, and want of sense.

Let duller fools on whom kind chance
   Some easy heart has thrown,
Despairing higher to advance,
   Be kind to one alone.

Old men and weak, whose idle flame,
   Their own defects discovers,
Since changing can but spread their shame,
   Ought to be constant lovers,

But we, whose hearts do justly swell
   With no vain-glorious pride,
Who know how we in love excel,
   Long to be often tried.

Then bring my bath and strew my bed,
   As each kind night returns:
I'll change a mistress till I'm dead,
   And fate change me for worms.

John Wilmot, Lord Rochester (1647–1680)

10 MAY

A Dedication to My Wife

To whom I owe the leaping delight
That quickens my senses in our wakingtime
And the rhythm that governs the repose of our sleepingtime,
    The breathing in unison

Of lovers whose bodies smell of each other
Who think the same thoughts without need of speech
And babble the same speech without need of meaning.

No peevish winter wind shall chill
No sullen tropic sun shall wither
The roses in the rose-garden which is ours and ours only

But this dedication is for others to read:
These are private words addressed to you in public.

T. S. Eliot (1888–1965)

11 MAY

Sonnet XXIV. Willowwood

PART I

I sat with Love upon a woodside well,
  Leaning across the water, I and he;
  Nor ever did he speak nor looked at me,
But touched his lute wherein was audible
The certain secret thing he had to tell:
  Only our mirrored eyes met silently
  In the low wave; and that sound came to be
The passionate voice I knew; and my tears fell.

And at their fall, his eyes beneath grew hers;
And with his foot and with his wing-feathers
  He swept the spring that watered my heart's drouth.
Then the dark ripples spread to waving hair,
And as I stooped, her own lips rising there
  Bubbled with brimming kisses at my mouth.

D. G. Rossetti (1828–1882)

12 MAY

New Love, New Life

I
She, who so long has lain
　Stone-stiff with folded wings,
Within my heart again
　The brown bird wakes and sings.

Brown nightingale, whose strain
　Is heard by day, by night,
She sings of joy and pain,
　Of sorrow and delight.

II
'Tis true, – in other days
　Have I unbarred the door;
He knows the walks and ways –
　Love has been here before.

Love blest and love accurst
　Was here in days long past;
This time is not the first,
　But this time is the last.

Amy Levy (1861–1889)

13 MAY

Sonnet LXXI
FROM *AMORETTI*

I joy to see how in your drawen work,
  Your selfe unto the Bee ye doe compare;
  and me unto the Spyder that doth lurke,
  in close awayt to catch her unaware.
Right so your selfe were caught in cunning snare
  of a deare for, and thralled to his love:
  in whose streight bands ye now captived are
  so firmely, that ye never may remove.
But as your whole worke is woven all above,
  with woodbynd flowers and fragrant Eglantine:
  so sweet your prison you in time shall prove,
  with many deare delights bedecked fyne,
And all thensforth eternall peace shall see
  betweene the Spyder and the gentle Bee.

Edmund Spenser (c.1552–1599)

14 MAY

Louisa

AFTER ACCOMPANYING HER ON A MOUNTAIN EXCURSION
WRITTEN AT TOWN-END, GRASSMERE.

I met Louisa in the shade,
And, having seen that lovely Maid,
Why should I fear to say
That, nymph-like, she is fleet and strong.
And down the rocks can leap along
Like rivulets in May?

She loves her fire, her cottage-home;
Yet o'er the moorland will she roam
In weather rough and bleak;
And, when against the wind she strains,
Oh! might I kiss the mountain rains
That sparkle on her cheek.

Take all that's mine "beneath the moon,"
If I with her but half a noon
May sit beneath the walls
Of some old cave, or mossy nook,
When up she winds along the brook
To hunt the waterfalls.

William Wordsworth (1770–1850)

15 MAY

The Night Has a Thousand Eyes

The night has a thousand eyes,
    And the day but one;
Yet the light of the bright world dies
    With the dying sun.

The mind has a thousand eyes,
    And the heart but one;
Yet the light of a whole life dies
    When love is done.

Francis William Bourdillon (1852–1921)

16 MAY

Bedouin Song

From the Desert I come to thee
On a stallion shod with fire;
And the winds are left behind
In the speed of my desire.
Under thy window I stand,
And the midnight hears my cry:
I love thee, I love but thee,
With a love that shall not die

Till the sun grows cold,
And the stars are old,
And the leaves of the Judgment Book Unfold!

Look from thy window and see
My passion and my pain;
I lie on the sands below,
And I faint in thy disdain.
Let the night-winds touch thy brow
With the heat of my burning sigh,
And melt thee to hear the vow
Of a love that shall not die

Till the sun grows cold,
And the stars are old,
And the leaves of the Judgment Book Unfold!

My steps are nightly driven,
By the fever in my breast,
To hear from thy lattice breathed
The word that shall give me rest.
Open the door of thy heart,
And open thy chamber door,
And my kisses shall teach thy lips
The love that shall fade no more

Till the sun grows cold,
And the stars are old,
And the leaves of the Judgment Book Unfold!

Bayard Taylor (1825–1878)

17 MAY

To Chloe

There are two births; the one when light
   First strikes the new awaken'd sense;
The other when two souls unite,
   And we must count our life from thence:
When you loved me and I loved you
Then both of us were born anew.

Love then to us new souls did give
   And in those souls did plant new powers;
Since when another life we live,
   The breath we breathe is his, not ours:
Love makes those young whom age doth chill,
And whom he finds young keeps young still.

William Cartwright (1611–1643)

18 MAY

On her Dancing

I stood and saw my Mistress dance,
Silent, and with so fixed an eye,
Some might suppose me in a trance:
   But being askèd why,
By one I who knew I was in love,
   I could not but impart
My wonder, to behold her move
So nimbly with a marble heart.

James Shirley (1596–1666)

19 MAY

Now Long Ago

One innocent spring
your voice meant to me
less than tires turning
on a distant street.

Your name, perhaps spoken,
led no chorus of
batons
unrehearsed
to crush against my
empty chest.

That cool spring
was shortened by
your summer, bold impatient
and all forgotten
except when silence
turns the key
into my midnight bedroom
and comes to sleep upon your
pillow.

Maya Angelou (1928–2014)

20 MAY

Love Is Enough

Love is enough. Let us not ask for gold.
  Wealth breeds false aims, and pride and selfishness;
In those serene, Arcadian days of old
  Men gave no thought to princely homes and dress.
The gods who dwelt on fair Olympia's height
Lived only for dear love and love's delight.
                              Love is enough.

Love is enough. Why should we care for fame?
  Ambition is a most unpleasant guest:
It lures us with the glory of a name
  Far from the happy haunts of peace and rest.
Let us stay here in this secluded place
Made beautiful by love's endearing grace!
                              Love is enough.

Love is enough. Why should we strive for power?
   It brings men only envy and distrust.
The poor world's homage pleases but an hour,
   And earthly honours vanish in the dust.
The proudest kinds are ofttimes desolate;
Let me be loved, and let who will be great.
                                     Love is enough.

Love is enough. Why should we ask for more?
   What greater gift have gods vouchsafed to men?
What better boon of all their precious store
   Than our fond hearts, that love and love again?
Old love may die; new love is just as sweet;
And life is fair and all the world complete:
                                     Love is enough.

Ella Wheeler Wilcox (1850–1919)

21 MAY

Judge nothing before the time

Love understands the mystery, whereof
   We can but spell a surface history:
Love knows, remembers: let us trust in Love:
   Love understands the mystery.

   Love weighs the event, the long pre-history,
Measures the depth beneath, the height above,
   The mystery, with the ante-mystery.

To love and to be grieved befits a dove
   Silently telling her bead-history:
Trust all to Love, be patient and approve:
   Love understands the mystery.

Christina Rossetti (1830–1894)

22 MAY

One to Love

Oh, where's the maid that I can love,
   With love which I have never told?
Where is the one that I would like
   To comfort me when I am old?

Do I not see before my face,
   A mate prepared for every one?
Then sure there's one prepared for me,
   Nor need I trudge the road alone.

Now who is he that speaks to me
   Of Mormons and of Mormonhood?
While this you know, the Lord has said,
   They twain shall be one flesh, one blood!

Come listen, then, to what I say
   Before this evening's work is done,
That you can do as you may please,
   But I'd be satisfied with one.

Islay Walden (1847–1884)

23 MAY

Interior

It sheds a shy solemnity,
This lamp in our poor room.
O grey and gold amenity,–
Silence and gentle gloom!

Wide from the world, a stolen hour
We claim, and none may know
How love blooms like a tardy flower
Here in the day's after-glow.

And even should the world break in
With jealous threat and guile,
The world, at last, must bow and win
Our pity and a smile.

Hart Crane (1899–1932)

24 MAY

'somewhere i have never travelled, gladly beyond'

somewhere i have never travelled,gladly beyond
any experience, your eyes have their silence:
in your most frail gesture are things which enclose me,
or which i cannot touch because they are too near

your slightest look easily will unclose me
though i have closed myself as fingers,
you open always petal by petal myself as Spring opens
(touching skillfully,mysteriously)her first rose

or if your wish be to close me,i and
my life will shut very beautifully, suddenly,
as when the heart of this flower imagines
the snow carefully everywhere descending;

nothing which we are to perceive in this world equals
the power of your intense fragility:whose texture
compels me with the colour of its countries,
rendering death and forever with each breathing

(i do not know what it is about you that closes
and opens;only something in me understands
the voice of your eyes is deeper than all roses)
nobody,not even the rain,has such small hands

e.e. cummings (1894–1962)

25 MAY

A Quoi Bon Dire?

   Seventeen years ago you said
Something that sounded like Good-bye;
   And everybody thinks that you are dead,
      But I.

   So I, as I grow stiff and cold
To this and that say Good-bye too;
   And everybody sees that I am old
      But you.

   And one fine morning in a sunny lane
Some boy and girl will meet and kiss and swear
   That nobody can love their way again
      While over there
You will have smiled, I shall have tossed your hair.

Charlotte Mew (1869–1928)

26 MAY

Merciles Beaute

I: CAPTIVITY

Your yën two wol slee me sodenly,
I may the beautè of hem not sustene,
So woundeth hit through-out my herte kene.

And but your word wol helen hastily
My hertes wounde, whyl that hit is grene,
  Your yën two wol slee me sodenly,
  I may the beautè of hem not sustene,

Upon my trouthe I sey yow faithfully,
That ye ben of my lyf and deeth the queen;
For with my deeth the trouth shal be sene.
  Your yën two wol slee me sodenly,
  I may the beautè of hem not sustene,
  So woundeth hit through-out my herte kene.

Geoffrey Chaucer (c.1340–1400)

Yën = eyes

27 MAY

A Sprig of Rosemary

I cannot see your face.
When I think of you,
It is your hands which I see.
Your hands
Sewing,
Holding a book,
Resting for a moment on the sill of a window.
My eyes keep always the sight of your hands,
But my heart holds the sound of your voice,
And the soft brightness which is your soul.

Amy Lowell (1874–1925)

28 MAY

Song

How sweet I roam'd from field to field,
And tasted all the summer's pride,
Till I the Prince of Love beheld,
Who in the sunny beams did glide!

He show'd me lilies for my hair,
And blushing roses for my brow;
He led me through his gardens fair,
Where all his golden pleasures grow.

With sweet May dews my wings were wet,
And Phoebus fir'd my vocal rage;
He caught me in his silken net,
And shut me in his golden cage.

He loves to sit and hear me sing,
Then, laughing, sports and plays with me;
Then stretches out my golden wing,
And mocks my loss of liberty.

William Blake (1757–1827)

29 MAY

Nuptials

River, be their teacher,
that together they may turn
their future highs and lows
into one hopeful flow

Two opposite shores
feeding from a single source.

Mountain, be their milestone,
that hand in hand they rise above
familiarity's worn tracks
into horizons of their own

Two separate footpaths
dreaming of a common peak.

Birdsong, be their mantra,
that down the frail aisles of their days,
their twilight hearts twitter morning
and their dreams prove branch enough.

John Agard (b.1949)

30 MAY

Sonnet LXI

Since there's no help, come let us kiss and part –
Nay, I have done: you get no more of me;
And I am glad, yea glad with all my heart,
That thus so cleanly I myself can free.
Shake hands for ever, cancel all our vows,
And when we meet at any time again,
Be it not seen in either of our brows
That we one jot of former love retain.
Now at the last gasp of love's latest breath,
When, his pulse failing, passion speechless lies;
When faith is kneeling by his bed of death,
And innocence is closing up his eyes,
    Now, if thou wouldst, when all have given him over,
    From death to life thou mightst him yet recover!

Michael Drayton (1563–1631)

31 MAY

XXXVIII

FROM *SONNETS FROM THE PORTUGUESE*

First time he kissed me, he but only kissed
The fingers of this hand wherewith I write,
And ever since it grew more clean and white,...
Slow to world-greetings, quick with its 'Oh, list,'
When the angels speak. A ring of amethyst
I could not wear here plainer to my sight,
Than that first kiss. The second passed in height
The first, and sought the forehead, and half missed,
Half falling on the hair. O beyond meed!
That was the chrism of love, which love's own crown,
With sanctifying sweetness, did precede.
The third, upon my lips, was folded down
In perfect, purple state! since when, indeed,
I have been proud and said, 'My Love, my own.'

Elizabeth Barrett Browning (1806–1861)

JUNE

All Thoughts, All Passions

1 JUNE

Alone

The lilies clustered fair and tall;
I stood outside the garden wall;
I saw her light robe glimmering through
The fragrant evening's dusk and dew.

She stopped above the lilies pale;
Up the clear east the moon did sail;
I saw her bend her lovely head
O'er her rich roses blushing red.

Her slender hand the flowers caressed,
Her touch the unconscious blossoms blessed;
The rose against her perfumed palm
Leaned its soft cheek in blissful calm.

I would have given my soul to be
That rose she touched so tenderly!
I stood alone, outside the gate,
And knew that life was desolate.

Celia Thaxter (1835–1894)

2 JUNE

Song

Two wedded lovers watched the rising moon,
    That with her strange mysterious beauty glowing,
    Over misty hills and waters flowing,
Crowned the long twilight loveliness of June:
    And thus in me, and thus in me, they spake,
    The solemn secret of first love did wake.

Above the hills the blushing orb arose;
    Her shape encircled by a radiant bower,
    In which the nightingale with charmèd power
Poured forth enchantment o'er the dark repose:
    And thus in me, and thus in me, they said,
    Earth's mists did with the sweet new spirit wed.

Far up the sky with ever purer beam,
    Upon the throne of night the moon was seated,
    And down the valley glens the shades retreated,
And silver light was on the open stream.
    And thus in me, and thus in me, they sighed,
    Aspiring Love has hallowed Passion's tide.

George Meredith (1828–1909)

3 JUNE

This and That

In this early dancing of a new day –
dogs leaping on the beach,
dolphins leaping not far from shore –
someone is bending over me,
is kissing me slowly.

Mary Oliver (1935–2019)

4 JUNE

No One so Much as You
VERSES 1–3

No one so much as you
Loves this my clay,
Or would lament as you
Its dying day.

You know me through and through
Though I have not told,
And though with what you know
You are not bold.

None ever was so fair
As I thought you:
Not a word can I bear
Spoken against you.

Edward Thomas (1878–1917)

5 JUNE

Song

Under the lime tree, on the daisied ground,
   Two that I know of made their bed;
There you may see, heaped and scattered round,
   Grass and blossoms, broken and shed,
All in a thicket down in the dale;
       Tandaradei –
Sweetly sang the nightingale.

Ere I set foot in the meadow, already
   Some one was waiting for somebody;
There was a meeting – Oh! gracious lady,
   There is no pleasure again for me.
Thousands of kisses there he took,
       Tandaradei –
See my lips, how red they look!

Leaf and blossom he had pulled and piled
   For a couch, a green one, soft and high;
And many a one hath gazed and smiled,
   Passing the bower and pressed grass by:
And the roses crushed hath seen –
       Tandaradei –
Where I laid my head between.

In this love-passage, if any one had been there,
   How sad and shamed should I be!
But what were we a doing alone among the green there,
   No soul shall ever know except my love and me,
And the little nightingale. –
      Tandaradei –
She, I wot, will tell no tale.

Walther von der Vogelweide (c.1170 – c.1230)
translated by **Thomas Lovell Beddoes (1803–1849)**

6 JUNE

Love without Hope

Love without hope, as when the young bird-catcher
Swept off his tall hat to the Squire's own daughter,
So let the imprisoned larks escape and fly
Singing about her head, as she rode by.

Robert Graves (1895–1985)

7 JUNE

The Spirit of Earth

Love me – and I will give into your hands
The rare, enamelled jewels of my lands,
Flowers red and blue,
Tender with air and dew.

From far green armouries of pools and meres
I'll reach for you my lucent sheaves of spears –
The singing falls,
Where the lone ousel calls.

When, like a passing light upon the sea,
Your wood-bird soul shall clap her wings and flee,
She shall but nest
More closely in my breast.

Mary Webb (1881–1927)

8 JUNE

A Red, Red Rose

My luve is like a red, red rose
   That's newly sprung in June;
My luve is like the melodie
   That's sweetly play'd in tune.
As fair art thou, my bonie lass,
   So deep in luve am I,
And I will luve thee still, my dear,
   Till a' the seas gang dry.

Till a' the seas gang dry, my dear,
   And the rocks melt wi' the sun!
I will luve thee still, my dear,
   While the sands o' life shall run.
And fare-thee-weel, my only luve,
   And fare-thee-weel a while!
And I will come again, my luve,
   Tho' it were ten-thousand mile.

Robert Burns (1759–1796)

9 JUNE

June Bracken and Heather
To –

There on the top of the down,
The wild heather round me and over me June's high blue,
When I look'd down at the bracken so bright and the
   heather so brown,
I thought to myself I would offer this book to you,
This, and my love together,
To you that are seventy-seven,
With a faith as clear as the heights of the June-blue heaven,
And a fancy as summer-new
As the green of the bracken amid the gloom of the heather.

Alfred, Lord Tennyson (1809–1892)

10 JUNE

Sonnet LXXV

FROM *AMORETTI*

One day I wrote her name upon the strand,
    But came the waves and washed it away:
    Again I wrote it with a second hand,
    But came the tide, and made my pains his prey.
Vain man, said she, that dost in vain assay,
    A mortal thing so to immortalize
    For I myself shall like to this decay,
    And eke my name be wiped out likewise.
Not so, (quod I) let baser things devise
    To die in dust, but you shall live by fame:
    My verse your vertues rare shall eternize,
    And in the heavens write your glorious name:
Where whereas Death shall all the world subdue,
    Our love shall live, and later life renew.

Edmund Spenser (c.1552–1599)

11 JUNE

A Welcome

LINES 1–4

Come in the evening, or come in the morning;
Come when you're looked for, or come without warning:
Kisses and welcome you'll find here before you,
And the oftener you come here the more I'll adore you.

Thomas O. Davis (1814–1845)

12 JUNE

Love Poem

I live in you, you live in me;
We are two gardens haunted by each other.
Sometimes I cannot find you there,
There is only the swing creaking, that you have just left,
Or your favourite book beside the sundial.

Douglas Dunn (b.1942)

13 JUNE

Hawthorn and Lavender XXII

Between the dusk of a summer night
   And the dawn of a summer day,
We caught at a mood as it passed in flight,
   And we bade it stoop and stay.
And what with the dawn of night began
   With the dusk of day was done;
For that is the way of woman and man,
   When a hazard has made them one.

Arc upon arc, from shade to shine,
   The World went thundering free;
And what was his errand but hers and mine –
   The lords of him, I and she?
O, it's die we must, but it's live we can,
   And the marvel of earth and sun
Is all for the joy of woman and man
   And the longing that makes them one.

W. E. Henley (1849–1903)

14 JUNE

Love is Not All (Sonnet XXX)

Love is not all: it is not meat or drink
Nor slumber nor a roof against the rain;
Nor yet a floating spar to men that sink
And rise and sink and rise and sink again;
Love cannot fill the thickened lung with breath,
Nor clean the blood, nor set the fractured bone;
Yet many a man is making friends with death
Even as I speak, for lack of love alone.
It may well be that in a difficult hour,
Pinned down by pain and moaning for release,
Or nagged by want past resolution's power,
I might be driven to sell your love for peace,
Or trade the memory of this night for food.
It may well be. I do not think I would.

Edna St Vincent Millay (1892–1950)

15 JUNE

Things base and vile

FROM *A MIDSUMMER NIGHT'S DREAM*, ACT I, SCENE I

Things base and vile, holding no quantity,
Love can transpose to form and dignity.
Love looks not with the eyes, but with the mind
And therefore is winged Cupid painted blind.
Nor hath love's mind of any judgement taste;
Wings and no eyes figure unheedy haste.
And therefore is love said to be a child
Because in choice he is so oft beguiled.

William Shakespeare (1564–1616)

16 JUNE

XLIII

FROM *SONNETS FROM THE PORTUGUESE*

How do I love thee? Let me count the ways.
I love thee to the depth and breadth and height
My soul can reach, when feeling out of sight
For the ends of Being and ideal Grace.
I love thee to the level of everyday's
Most quiet need, by sun and candle-light.
I love thee freely, as men strive for Right;
I love thee purely, as they turn from Praise.
I love thee with the passion put to use
In my old griefs, and with my childhood's faith.
I love thee with a love I seemed to lose
With my lost saints,– I love thee with the breath,
Smiles, tears, of all my life!– and, if God choose,
I shall but love thee better after death.

Elizabeth Barrett Browning (1806–1861)

17 JUNE

Out of this Love

Out of this love
the light arises.
Energy blossoms into meaning:
people dance and sing,
flowers bloom,
and fields and hills have life.

So spirit flowers,
and God is known;
and blessedness is born –
and love – in all its forms.

David Austin (1926–2018)

18 JUNE

A Bed of Forget-me-nots

Is love so prone to change and rot
We are fain to rear forget-me-not
By measure in a garden plot? –

I love its growth at large and free
By untrod path and unlopped tree,
Or nodding by the unpruned hedge,
Or on the water's dangerous edge
Where flags and meadowsweet blow rank
With rushes on the quaking bank.

Love is not taught in learning's school,
Love is not parcelled out by rule;
Hath curb or call an answer got? –
So free must be forget-me-not.
Give me the flame no dampness dulls,
The passion of the instinctive pulse,
Love steadfast as a fixèd star,
Tender as doves with nestlings are,
More large than time, more strong than death:
This all creation travails of –
She groans not for a passing breath–
This is forget-me-not and love.

Christina Rossetti (1830–1884)

19 JUNE

Song

The lark now leaves his watery nest,
   And climbing, shakes his dewy wings;
He takes this window for the east,
   And to implore your light, he sings,
Awake, awake, the morn will never rise,
Till she can dress her beauty at your eyes.

The merchant bows unto the seaman's star,
   The ploughman from the sun his season takes;
But still the lover wonders what they are,
   Who look for day before his mistress wakes.
Awake, awake, break through your veils of lawn!
Then draw your curtains, and begin the dawn.

Sir William Davenant (1572–1641)

20 JUNE

Love

VERSES 1-3

All thoughts, all passions, all delights,
Whatever stirs this mortal frame,
All are but ministers of Love,
    And feed his sacred flame.

Oft in my waking dreams do I
Live o'er again that happy hour,
When midway on the mount I lay,
    Beside the ruined tower.

The moonshine, stealing o'er the scene
Had blended with the lights of eve;
And she was there, my hope, my joy,
    My own dear Genevieve!

Samuel Taylor Coleridge (1772-1834)

21 JUNE

Flowers

Some men never think of it.
You did. You'd come along
And say you'd nearly brought me flowers
But something had gone wrong.

The shop was closed. Or you had doubts –
The sort that minds like ours
Dream up incessantly. You thought
I might not want your flowers..

It made me smile and hug you then.
Now I can only smile.
But, look, the flowers you nearly brought
Have lasted all this while.

Wendy Cope (b.1945)

22 JUNE

Dover Beach

The sea is calm tonight.
The tide is full, the moon lies fair
Upon the straits; – on the French coast the light
Gleams and is gone; the cliffs of England stand,
Glimmering and vast, out in the tranquil bay.
Come to the window, sweet is the night air!
Only, from the long line of spray
Where the sea meets the moon-blanch'd land,
Listen! you hear the grating roar
Of pebbles which the waves draw back, and fling,
At their return, up the high strand,
Begin, and cease, and then again begin,
With tremulous cadence slow, and bring
The eternal note of sadness in.

Sophocles long ago
Heard it on the Ægæan, and it brought
Into his mind the turbid ebb and flow
Of human misery; we
Find also in the sound a thought,
Hearing it by this distant northern sea.

The Sea of Faith
Was once, at the full, and round earth's shore
Lay like the folds of a bright girdle furl'd.
But now I only hear
Its melancholy, long, withdrawing roar,
Retreating, to the breath
Of the night-wind, down the vast edges drear
And naked shingles of this world.

Ah, love, let us be true
To one another! for the world, which seems
To lie before us like a land of dreams,
So various, so beautiful, so new,
Hath really neither joy, nor love, nor light,
Nor certitude, nor peace, nor help for pain;
And we are here as on a darkling plain
Swept with confused alarms of struggle and flight,
Where ignorant armies clash by night.

Matthew Arnold (1822–1888)

23 JUNE

Ballad

Fair maiden when my love began
Ere though thy beauty knew
I fearless owned my passion then
Nor met reproof from you

But now perfection wakes thy charms
And strangers turn to praise
Thy pride my faint-grown heart alarms
And I scarce dare to gaze

Those lips to which mine own did grow
In love's glad infancy
With ruby ripeness now doth glow
As gems too rich for me

The full-blown rose thy cheeks doth wear
Those lilys on thy brow
Forget whose kiss their buds did wear
And bloom above me now

Those eyes whose first sweet timid light
Did my young hopes inspire
Like midday suns in splendour bright
Now burn me with their fire

Nor can I weep what I bemoan
As great as are my fears
Too burning is my passion grown
To o'er be quenched by tears

John Clare (1793–1864)

24 JUNE

Song

   Go, lovely rose!
Tell her that wastes her time and me,
   That now she knows,
When I resemble her to thee,
How sweet and fair she seems to be.

   Tell her that's young,
And shuns to have her graces spied,
   That hadst thou sprung
In deserts, where no men abide,
Thou must have uncommended died.

   Small is the worth
Of beauty from the light retired;
   Bid her come forth,
Suffer herself to be desired,
And not blush so to be admired.

   Then die! that she
The common fate of all things rare
   May read in thee;
How small a part of time they share
That are so wondrous sweet and fair!

Edmund Waller (1606–1687)

25 JUNE

In Paris with You

Don't talk to me of love. I've had an earful
And I get tearful when I've downed a drink or two.
I'm one of your talking wounded.
I'm a hostage. I'm maroonded.
But I'm in Paris with you.

Yes I'm angry at the way I've been bamboozled
And resentful at the mess I've been through.
I admit I'm on the rebound
And I don't care where are *we* bound.
I'm in Paris with you.

Do you mind if we do *not* go to the Louvre
If we say sod off to sodding Notre Dame,
If we skip the Champs Elysées
And remain here in this sleazy

Old hotel room
Doing this and that
To what and whom
Learning who you are,
Learning what I am.

Don't talk to me of love. Let's talk of Paris,
The little bit of Paris in our view.
There's that crack across the ceiling
And the hotel walls are peeling
And I'm in Paris with you.

Don't talk to me of love. Let's talk of Paris.
I'm in Paris with the slightest thing you do.
I'm in Paris with your eyes, your mouth,
I'm in Paris with... all points south.
Am I embarrassing you?
I'm in Paris with you.

James Fenton (b.1949)

26 JUNE

Summer Night, Riverside

In the wild soft summer darkness
How many and many a night we two together
Sat in the park and watched the Hudson
Wearing her lights like golden spangles
Glinting on black satin.
The rail along the curving pathway
Was low in a happy place to let us cross,
And down the hill a tree that dripped with bloom
Sheltered us,
While your kisses and the flowers,
Falling, falling,
Tangled in my hair....

The frail white stars moved slowly over the sky.

And now, far off
In the fragrant darkness
The tree is tremulous again with bloom
For June comes back.

To-night what girl
Dreamily before her mirror shakes from her hair
This year's blossoms, clinging to its coils?

Sara Teasdale (1884–1933)

27 JUNE

As I walked out one Evening
VERSES 1–5

As I walked out one evening,
   Walking down Bristol Street,
The crowds upon the pavement
   Were fields of harvest wheat.

And down by the brimming river
   I heard a lover sing
Under an arch of the railway:
   'Love has no ending.

'I'll love you, dear, I'll love you
   Till China and Africa meet,
And the river jumps over the mountain
   And the salmon sing in the street,

'I'll love you till the ocean
   Is folded and hung up to dry
And the seven stars go squawking
   Like geese about the sky.

'The years shall run like rabbits,
   For in my arms I hold
The Flower of the Ages,
   And the first love of the world.'

W. H. Auden (1907–1973)

28 JUNE

To the Virgins, to Make Much of Time

Gather ye Rose-buds while ye may,
   Old Time is still a flying;
And this same flower that smiles today
   To morrow will be dying.

The glorious Lamp of Heaven, the Sun,
   The higher he's a-getting,
The sooner will his Race be run,
   And nearer he's to Setting.

That Age is best, which is the first,
   When Youth and Blood are warmer;
But being spent, the worse, and worst
   Times, still succeed the former.

Then be not coy, but use your time;
   And while ye may, goe marry;
For having lost but once your prime,
   You may forever tarry.

Robert Herrick (1591–1674)

29 JUNE

At Bay St. Louis

Soft breezes blow and swiftly show
   Through fragrant orange branches parted,
A maiden fair, with sun-flecked hair,
   Caressed by arrows, golden darted.
The vine-clad tree holds forth to me
   A promise sweet of purple blooms,
And chirping bird, scarce seen but heard
   Sings dreamily, and sweetly croons
     At Bay St. Louis.

The hammock swinging, idly singing,
   Lissome nut-brown maid
   Swings gaily, freely, to-and-fro;
The curling, green-white waters casting cool, clear shade,
   Rock small, shell boats that go
In circles wide, or tug at anchor's chain,
As though to skim the sea with cargo vain,
     At Bay St. Louis.

   The maid swings slower, slower to-and-fro,
And sunbeams kiss gray, dreamy half-closed eyes;
   Fond lover creeping on with foot steps slow,
Gives gentle kiss, and smiles at sweet surprise.
    . . . . . .
   The lengthening shadows tell that eve is nigh,
   And fragrant zephyrs cool and calmer grow,
Yet still the lover lingers, and scarce breathed sigh,
   Bids the swift hours to pause, nor go,
     At Bay St. Louis.

Alice Dunbar Nelson (1875–1935)

30 JUNE

XVIII

FROM *CHAMBER MUSIC*

O Sweetheart, hear you
   Your lover's tale;
A man shall have sorrow
   When friends him fail.

For he shall know then
   Friends be untrue
And a little ashes
   Their words come to.

But one unto him
   Will softly move
And softly woo him
   In ways of love.

His hand is under
   Her smooth round breast;
So he who has sorrow
   Shall have rest.

James Joyce (1882–1941)

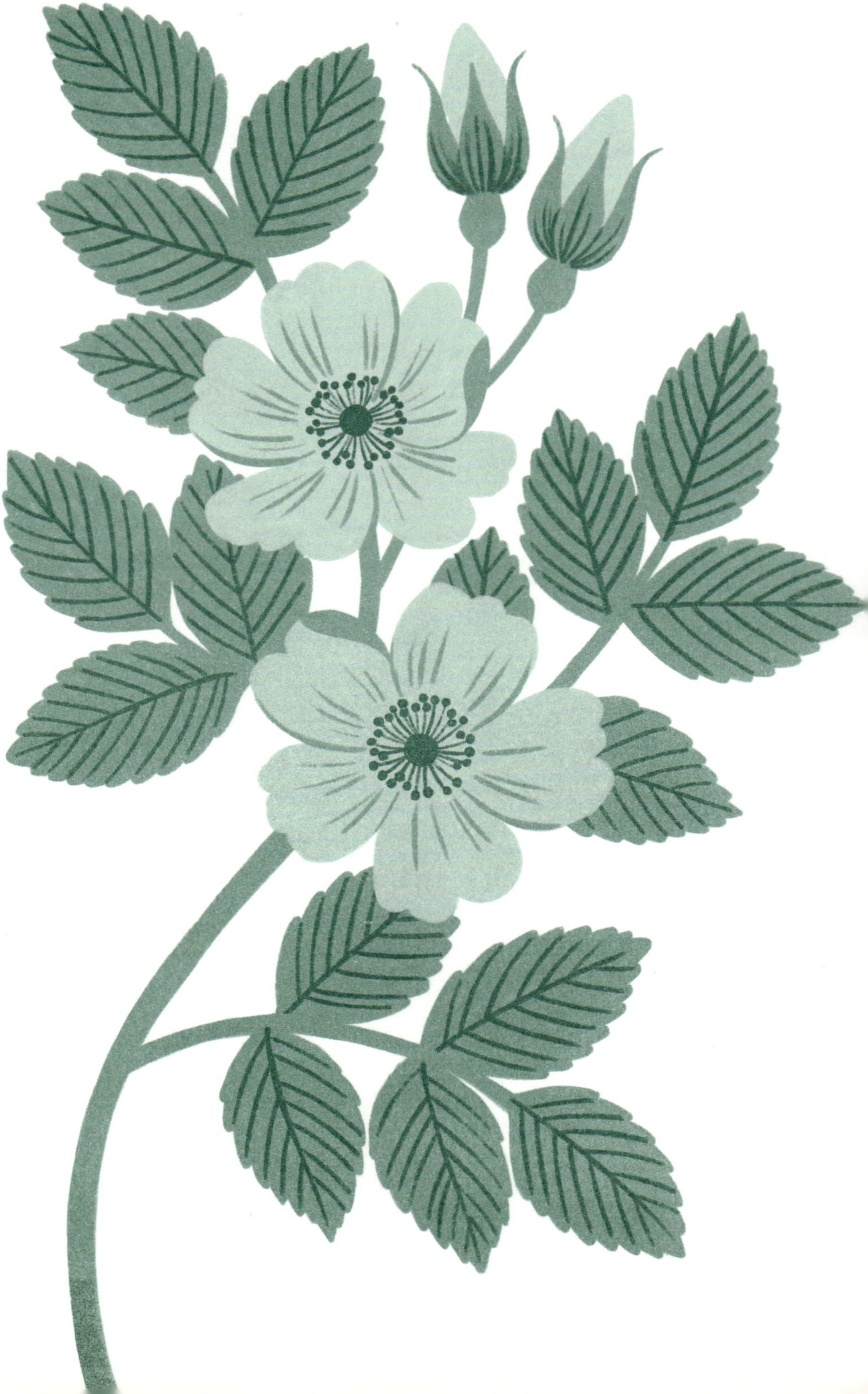

JULY

Two Hearts Beating

1 JULY

Sonnet 18

Shall I compare thee to a summer's day?
Thou art more lovely and more temperate:
Rough winds do shake the darling buds of May,
And summer's lease hath all too short a date;
Sometime too hot the eye of heaven shines,
And often is his gold complexion dimmed;
And every fair from fair sometime declines,
By chance or nature's changing course untrimmed;
But thy eternal summer shall not fade,
Nor lose possession of that fair thou ow'st;
Nor shall death brag thou wander'st in his shade,
When in eternal lines to time thou grow'st:
   So long as men can breathe or eyes can see,
   So long lives this, and this gives life to thee.

William Shakespeare (1564–1616)

2 JULY

XIII

FROM *A SHROPSHIRE LAD*

When I was one-and-twenty
    I heard a wise man say,
'Give crowns and pounds and guineas
    But not your heart away;
Give pearls away and rubies
    But keep your fancy free.'
But I was one-and-twenty,
    No use to talk to me.

When I was one-and-twenty
    I heard him say again,
'The heart out of the bosom
    Was never given in vain;
'Tis paid with sighs a plenty
    And sold for endless rue.'
And I am two-and-twenty,
    And oh, 'tis true, 'tis true.

A. E. Housman (1859–1936)

3 JULY

Sonnet LI
SUPPOSED TO HAVE BEEN WRITTEN IN THE HEBRIDES

On this lone island, whose unfruitful breast
   Feeds but the summer-shepherd's little flock
   With scanty herbage from the half-clothed rock,
Where ospreys, cormorants, and sea-mews rest;
   Even in a scene so desolate and rude
I could with *thee* for months and years be blest;
And of thy tenderness and love possest,
   Find all *my* world in this wild solitude!
When summer suns these northern seas illume,
   With thee admire the light's reflected charms,
And when drear winter spreads his cheerless gloom,
Still find Elysium in thy shelt'ring arms:
For thou to me canst sovereign bliss impart,
Thy mind my empire – and my throne thy heart.

Charlotte Smith (1749–1806)

4 JULY

Sonnet VII

Like an enfranchised bird, who wildly springs,
   With a keen sparkle in his glancing eye
And a strong effort in his quivering wings,
   Up to the blue vault of the happy sky, –
So my enamour'd heart, so long thine own,
   At length from Love's imprisonment set free.
Goes forth into the open world alone,
   Glad and exulting in its liberty:
But like that helpless bird, (confined so long,
   His weary wings have lost all power to soar,)
Who soon forgets to trill his joyous song,
   And, feebly fluttering, sinks to earth once more, –
So, from its former bonds released in vain,
My heart still feels the weight of that remember'd chain.

Caroline Norton (1808–1877)

5 JULY

Elegia V
CORINNAE CONCUBITUS

In summer's heat and mid-time of the day
To rest my limbs upon a bed I lay,
One window shut, the other open stood,
Which gave such light as twinkles in a wood,
Like twilight glimpse at setting of the sun
Or night being past, and yet not day begun.
Such light to shamefaced maidens must be shown,
Where they may sport, and seem to be unknown.
Then came Corinna in a long loose gown,
Her white neck hid with tresses hanging down:
Resembling fair Semiramis going to bed
Or Lais of a thousand wooers sped.
I snatch'd her gown, being thin, the harm was small,
Yet striv'd she to be covered therewithal.
And striving thus as one that would be cast,
Betray'd herself, and yielded at the last.
Stark naked as she stood before mine eye,
Not one wen in her body could I spy.
What arms and shoulders did I touch and see,
How apt her breasts were to be press'd by me!
How smooth a belly under her waist saw I,
How large a leg, and what a lusty thigh!
To leave the rest, all lik'd me passing well,
I cling'd her naked body, down she fell,
Judge you the rest: being tir'd she bad me kiss,
Jove send me more such afternoons as this.

Ovid (43 BCE – 18 CE)
translated by **Christopher Marlowe (1564–1593)**

6 JULY

New Face

I have learned not to worry about love;
but to honor its coming
with all my heart.
To examine the dark mysteries
of the blood
with headless heed and
swirl,
to know the rush of feelings
swift and flowing
as water.
The source appears to be
some inexhaustible
spring
within our twin and triple
selves;
the new face I turn up
to you
no one else on earth
has ever
seen.

Alice Walker (b.1944)

7 JULY

To the Ladie Lucie, Countesse of Bedford

Me thinkes I see faire Virtue readie stand,
T'unlocke the closet of your lovely breast,
Holding the key of Knowledge in her hand,
Key of that Cabbine where your selfe doth rest,
To let him in, by whom her youth was blest:
   The true-love of your soule, your hearts delight,
   Fairer than all the world in your cleare sight.

He that descended from celestiall glory,
To taste of our infirmities and sorrowes,
Whose heavenly wisdom read the earthly storie
Of fraile Humanity, which his godhead borrows:
Loe here he coms all stucke with pale deaths arrows:
   In whose most pretious wounds your soule may reade
   Salvation, while he (dying Lord) doth bleed.

You whose cleare Judgement farre exceeds my skil,
Vouchsafe to entertaine this dying lover,
The Ocean of true grace, whose streames doe fill
All those with Joy, that can his love recover;
About this blessed Arke bright Angels hover:
   Where your faire soule may sure and safely rest,
   When he is sweetly seated in your brest.

There may your thoughts as servants to your heart,
Give true attendance on this lovely guest,
While he doth to that blessed bowre impart
Flowres of fresh comforts, decke that bed of rest,
With such rich beauties as may make it blest.
   And you in whom all raritie is found,
   May be with his eternall glory crownd.

Aemilia Lanyer (1569–1645)

8 JULY

Hawthorn and Lavender XXVII

It was a bowl of roses:
   There in the light they lay,
Languishing, glorying, glowing
   Their life away.

And the soul of them rose like a presence,
   Into me crept and grew,
And filled me with something – some one –
   O, was it you?

W. E. Henley (1849–1903)

9 JULY

Non sum qualis eram bonae sub regno Cynarae

Last night, ah, yesternight, betwixt her lips and mine
There fell thy shadow, Cynara! thy breath was shed
Upon my soul between the kisses and the wine;
And I was desolate and sick of an old passion,
   Yea, I was desolate and bowed my head:
I have been faithful to thee, Cynara! in my fashion.

All night upon mine heart I felt her warm heart beat,
Night-long within mine arms in love and sleep she lay;
Surely the kisses of her bought red mouth were sweet;
But I was desolate and sick of an old passion,
   When I awoke and found the dawn was gray:
I have been faithful to thee, Cynara! in my fashion.

I have forgot much, Cynara! gone with the wind,
Flung roses, roses riotously with the throng,
Dancing, to put thy pale, lost lilies out of mind,
But I was desolate and sick of an old passion,
   Yea, all the time, because the dance was long:
I have been faithful to thee, Cynara! in my fashion.

I cried for madder music and for stronger wine,
But when the feast is finished and the lamps expire,
Then falls thy shadow, Cynara! the night is thine;
And I am desolate and sick of an old passion,
   Yea, hungry for the lips of my desire:
I have been faithful to thee, Cynara! in my fashion.

Ernest Dowson (1867–1900)

10 JULY

I Know Someone

I know someone who kisses the way
a flower opens, but more rapidly.
Flowers are sweet. They have
short, beatific lives. They offer
much pleasure. There is
nothing in the world that can be said
against them.
Sad, isn't it, that all they can kiss
is the air.

Yes, yes! We are the lucky ones.

Mary Oliver (1935–2019)

11 JULY

Song

She is not fair to outward view
   As many maidens be,
Her loveliness I never knew
   Until she smil'd on me;
Oh! then I saw her eye was bright,
A well of love, a spring of light!

But now her looks are coy and cold,
   To mine they ne'er reply,
And yet I cease not to behold
   The love-light in her eye:
Her very frowns are fairer far
Than smiles of other maidens are.

Hartley Coleridge (1796–1849)

12 JULY

A Man Who Would Woo a Fair Maid

FROM *THE YEOMAN OF THE GUARD*, ACT II

A man who would woo a fair maid,
Should 'prentice himself to the trade;
  And study all day,
  In methodical way,
How to flatter, cajole, and persuade.
He should 'prentice himself at fourteen
And practise from morning to e'en;
  And when he's of age,
  If he will, I'll engage,
He may capture the heart of a queen!
    It is purely a matter of skill,
    Which all may attain if they will:
      But every Jack
      He must study the knack
    If he wants to make sure of his Jill!

If he's made the best use of his time,
His twig he'll so carefully lime
  That every bird
  Will come down at his word,
Whatever its plumage and clime.
He must learn that the thrill of a touch
May mean little, or nothing, or much;
  It's an instrument rare,
  To be handled with care,
And ought to be treated as such.

    It is purely a matter of skill,
      Which all may attain if they will:
        But every Jack,
        He must study the knack
      If he wants to make sure of his Jill!

Then a glance may be timid or free;
It will vary in mighty degree,
   From an impudent stare
   To a look of despair
That no maid without pity can see.
And a glance of despair is no guide –
It may have its ridiculous side;
   It may draw you a tear
   Or a box on the ear;
You can never be sure till you've tried.
    It is purely a matter of skill,
      Which all may attain if they will:
        But every Jack
        He must study the knack
      If he wants to make sure of his Jill!

W. S. Gilbert (1836–1911)

13 JULY

Sonnet for the Madonna of the Cherries

Dear Lady of the Cherries, cool, serene,
Untroubled by the follies, strife and fears,
Clad in soft reds and blues and mantle green
Your memory has been with me all these years.

Long years of battle, bitterness and waste,
Dry years of sun and dust and Eastern skies,
Hard years of ceaseless struggle, endless haste,
Fighting 'gainst greed for power hate and lies.

Your red-gold hair, your slowly smiling face
For pride in your dear son, your King of Kings,
Fruits of the kindly earth, and truth and grace,
Colour and light, and all warm lovely things –

   For all that lovelieness, that warmth, that light,
   Blessed Madonna, I go back to fight.

A. P. Wavell (1883–1950)

14 JULY

Miles Away

I want you and you are not here. I pause
in this garden, breathing the colour thought is
before language into still air. Even your name
is a pale ghost and, though I exhale it again
and again, it will not stay with me. Tonight
I make you up, imagine you, your movements clearer
than the words I have you say you said before.

Wherever you are now, inside my head you fix me
with a look, standing here whilst cool late light
dissolves into the earth. I have got your mouth wrong,
but still it smiles. I hold you closer, miles away,
inventing love, until the calls of nightjars
interrupt and turn what was to come, was certain,
into memory. The stars are filming us for no one.

Carol Ann Duffy (b.1955)

15 JULY

Song

FROM *MARRIAGE-À-LA-MODE*

1

Whil'st *Alexis* lay prest
In her Arms he lov'd best,
With his hands round her neck,
And his head on her breast,
He found the fierce pleasure too hasty to stay,
And his soul in the tempest just flying away.

2

When *Celia* saw this,
With a sigh, and a kiss,
She cry'd, 'Oh my dear, I am robb'd of my bliss;
'Tis unkind to your Love, and unfaithfully done,
To leave me behind you, and die all alone.'

3

The Youth, though in haste,
And breathing his last,
In pity dy'd slowly, while she dy'd more fast;
Till at length she cry'd, Now, my dear, now let us go;
Now die, my *Alexis*, and I will die too.

4

Thus intranc'd they did lie,
Till *Alexis* did try
To recover new breath, that again he might die:
Then often they di'd; but the more they did so,
The Nymph di'd more quick, and the Shepherd more slow.

John Dryden (1631–1700)

16 JULY

The Sunne Rising

    Busie old foole, unruly Sunne,
      Why dost thou thus,
Through windowes, and through curtaines call on us?
Must to thy motions lovers seasons run?
      Sawcy pedantique wretch, goe chide
        Late school boyes, and sowre prentices,
   Goe tell Court-huntsmen, that the King will ride,
   Call countrey ants to harvest offices;
Love, all alike, no season knowes, nor clyme,
Nor houres, dayes, months, which are the rags of time.

    Thy beames, so reverend, and strong
      Why shouldst thou thinke?
I could eclipse and cloud them with a winke,
But that I would not lose her sight so long:
      If her eyes have not blinded thine,
        Looke, and to morrow late, tell mee,
   Whether both the'India's of spice and Myne
   Be where thou leftst them, or lie here with mee.
Aske for those Kings whom thou saw'st yesterday,
And thou shalt heare, All here in one bed lay.

    She'is all States, and all Princes, I,
       Nothing else is.
Princes doe but play us; compar'd to this,
All honor's mimique; All wealth alchimie.
    Thou sunne art halfe as happy'as wee,
       In that the world's contracted thus;
   Thine age askes ease, and since thy duties bee
   To warme the world, that's done in warming us.
Shine here to us, and thou art everywhere;
This bed thy center is, these walls, thy spheare.

John Donne (1572–1631)

17 JULY

Gloire de Dijon

When she rises in the morning
I linger to watch her;
She spreads the bath-cloth underneath the window
And the sunbeams catch her
Glistening white on the shoulders,
While down her sides the mellow
Golden shadow glows as
She stoops to the sponge, and her swung breasts
Sway like full-blown yellow
Gloire de Dijon roses.

She drips herself with water, and her shoulders
Glisten as silver, they crumple up
Like wet and falling roses, and I listen
For the sluicing of their rain-dishevelled petals.
In the window full of sunlight
Concentrates her golden shadow
Fold on fold, until it glows as
Mellow as the glory roses.
Icking

D. H. Lawrence (1885–1930)

18 JULY

In a Bath Teashop

"Let us not speak, for the love we bear one another –
   Let us hold hands and look."
She, such a very ordinary little woman;
   He, such a thumping crook;
But both, for a moment, little lower than the angels
   In the teashop's ingle-nook.

John Betjeman (1906–1984)

19 JULY

To Celia

Come, my Celia, let us prove,
While we can, the sports of love;
Time will not be ours forever;
He at length our good will sever.
Spend not then his gifts in vain.
Suns that set may rise again;
But if once we lose this light,
'Tis with us perpetual night.
Why should we defer our joys?
Fame and rumour are but toys.
Cannot we delude the eyes
Of a few poor household spies,
Or his easier ears beguile,
So removed by our wile?
'Tis no sin love's fruit to steal;
But the sweet theft to reveal,
To be taken, to be seen,
These have crimes accounted been.

Ben Jonson (1572–1637)

20 JULY

Love for Love's Sake

I'll range around the shady bowers
And gather all the sweetest flowers;
I'll strip the garden and the grove
To make a garland for my love.

When in the sultry heat of day
My thirsty nymph does panting lay,
I'll hasten to the river's brink
And drain the floods, but she shall drink.

At night to rest her weary head
I'll make my love a grassy bed
And with green boughs I'll form a shade
That nothing may her rest invade.

And while dissolved in sleep she lies,
My self shall never close these eyes;
But gazing still with fond delight
I'll watch my charmer all the night.

And then as soon as cheerful day
Dispels the darksome shades away,
Forth to the forest I'll repair
To seek provision for my fair.

Thus will I spend the day and night,
Still mixing labour with delight,
Regarding nothing I endure
So I can ease for her procure.

But if the nymph whom thus I love
To her fond swain should faithless prove,
I'll seek some distant shore
And never think of woman more.

Henry Carey (1687–1743)

21 JULY

My Wife

Trusty, dusky, vivid, true,
With eyes of gold and bramble-dew,
Steel-true and blade-straight,
The great artificer
Made my mate.

Honour, anger, valour, fire;
A love that life could never tire,
Death quench or evil stir,
The mighty master
Gave to her.

Teacher, tender, comrade, wife,
A fellow-farer true through life,
Heart-whole and soul-free
The august father
Gave to me.

Robert Louis Stevenson (1850–1894)

22 JULY

At Baia

I should have thought
in a dream you would have brought
some lovely, perilous thing,
orchids piled in a great sheath,
as who would say (in a dream),
I send you this,
who left the blue veins
of your throat unkissed.

Why was it that your hands
(that never took mine),
your hands that I could see
drift over the orchid-heads
so carefully,
your hands, so fragile, sure to lift
so gently, the fragile flower-stuff –
ah, ah, how was it

You never sent (in a dream)
the very form, the very scent,
not heavy, not sensuous,
but perilous – perilous –
of orchids, piled in a great sheath,
and folded underneath on a bright scroll,
some word:

Flower sent to flower;
for white hands, the lesser white,
less lovely of flower-leaf,

or

Lover to lover, no kiss,
no touch, but forever and ever this.

H. D. / Hilda Doolittle (1886–1961)

23 JULY

The Change

Love in her Sunny Eyes does basking play;
   Love walks the pleasant Mazes of her Hair;
Love does on both her Lips for ever stray;
And *sows* and *reaps* a thousand *kisses* there.
In all her outward parts Love's always seen;
   But, oh, He never went within.

Within *Love's* foes, his greatest foes abide,
   Malice, Inconstancy, and Pride.
So the Earth's face, Trees, Herbs, and Flowers do dress,
   With other beauties numberless:
But at the *Center*, *Darkness* is, and *Hell*;
There wicked *Spirits*, and there the *Damned* dwell.

With me alas, quite contrary it fares;
Darkness and *Death* lies in my weeping eyes,
Despair and Paleness in my face appears,
And Grief, and Fear, Love's greatest Enemies;
But, like the Persian-Tyrant, Love within
   Keeps his proud Court, and ne're is seen.

Oh take *my Heart*, and by that means you'll prove
   Within, too stor'd enough of *Love*:
Give me but yours, I'll by that change so thrive,
   That *Love* in all my parts shall live.
So powerful is this change, it render can,
My *outside Woman*, and your *inside Man*.

Abraham Cowley (1618–1667)

24 JULY

Meeting at Night

I

The grey sea and the long black land;
And the yellow half-moon large and low;
And the startled little waves that leap
In fiery ringlets from their sleep,
As I gain the cove with pushing prow,
And quench its speed in the slushy sand.

II

Then a mile of warm sea-scented beach;
Three fields to cross till a farm appears;
A tap at the pane, the quick sharp scratch
And blue spurt of a lighted match,
And a voice less loud, thro' its joys and fears,
Than the two hearts beating each to each!

Robert Browning (1812–1889)

25 JULY

Paul to Virginia
FIN DE SIECLE

I really must confess, my dear,
    I cannot help but love you,
For of all girls I ever knew,
    There's none I place above you;
But then you know it's rather hard,
    To dangle aimless at your skirt,
And watch your every movement so,
    For I am jealous, and you're a flirt.

There's half a score of fellows round,
    You smile at every one,
And as I think to pride myself for basking in the sun
Of your sweet smiles, you laugh at me,
    And treat me like a lump of dirt,
Until I wish that I were dead,
    For I am jealous, and you're a flirt.

I'm sorry that I've ever known
    Your loveliness entrancing,
Or ever saw your laughing eyes,
    With girlish mischief dancing;
'Tis agony supreme and rare
To see your slender waist a-girt
With other fellows' arms, you see,
    For I am jealous, and you're a flirt.

Now, girlie, if you'll promise me,
    To never, never treat me mean,
I'll show you in a little while,
    The best sweetheart you've ever seen;
You do not seem to know or care,
    How often you've my feelings hurt,
While flying round with other boys,
    For I am jealous, and you're a flirt.

Alice Dunbar Nelson (1875–1935)

26 JULY

Aire and Angels

Twice or thrice had I loved thee,
Before I knew thy face or name;
So in a voice, so in a shapeless flame,
Angells affect us oft, and worshipp'd bee,
   Still when, to where thou wert, I came,
Some lovely glorious nothing I did see.
   But since, my soule, whose child love is,
Takes limmes of flesh, and else could nothing doe,
   More subtile than the parent is,
Love must not be, but take a body too,
   And therefore what thou wert, and who,
      I did Love ask, and now
That it assume thy body, I allow,
And fixe it selfe ino thy lip, eye, and brow.

Whilst thus to ballast love, I thought,
And so more steddily to have gone,
With wares which would sinke admiration,
I saw, I had loves pinnace overfraught
   Ev'ry thy haire for love to worke upon
Is much too much, some fitter must be sought;
   For, nor in nothing, nor in things
Extreme, and scattring bright, can love inhere;
   Then as an Angell, face, and wings
Of aire, not pure as it, yet pure doth weare,
   So thy love may be my loves spheare.
      Just such disparitie
As is 'twixt Aire and Angells puritie,
T'wixt womens love, and mens will ever bee.

John Donne (1572–1631)

27 JULY

I have no Life but this

I have no Life but this –
To lead it here –
Nor any Death – but lest
Dispelled from there –

Nor tie to Earths to come –
Nor Action new –
Except through this extent –
The Realm of you –

Emily Dickinson (1830–1886)

28 JULY

Tray, the Exemplar

My dog (the trustiest of his kind)
With gratitude inflames my mind;
I mark his true, his faithful way,
And in my service copy Tray.

John Gay (1685–1732)

29 JULY

Ballad of the Londoner

Evening falls on the smoky walls,
   And the railings drip with rain,
And I will cross the old river
   To see my girl again.

The great and solemn-gliding tram,
   Love's still-mysterious car,
Has many a light of gold and white.
   And a single dark red star.

I know a garden in a street
   Which no one ever knew;
I know a rose beyond the Thames,
   Where flowers are pale and few.

James Elroy Flecker (1884–1915)

30 JULY

Harlem Night Song

Come,
Let us roam the night together
Singing.

I love you.

Across
The Harlem roof-tops
Moon is shining
Night sky is blue.
Stars are great drops
Of golden dew.

Down the street
A band is playing.

I love you.

Come,
Let us roam the night together
Singing.

Langston Hughes (1901–1967)

31 JULY

Now sleeps the crimson petal

FROM *THE PRINCESS*, PART VII

Now sleeps the crimson petal, now the white;
Nor waves the cypress in the palace walk;
Nor winks the gold fin in the porphyry font:
The firefly wakens; waken thou with me.

Now droops the milk-white peacock like a ghost,
And like a ghost she glimmers on to me.

Now lies the Earth all Danaë to the stars,
And all thy heart lies open unto me.

Now slides the silent meteor on, and leaves
A shining furrow, as thy thoughts in me.

Now folds the lily all her sweetness up,
And slips into the bosom of the lake.
So fold thyself, my dearest, thou, and slip
Into my bosom and be lost in me.

Alfred, Lord Tennyson (1809–1892)

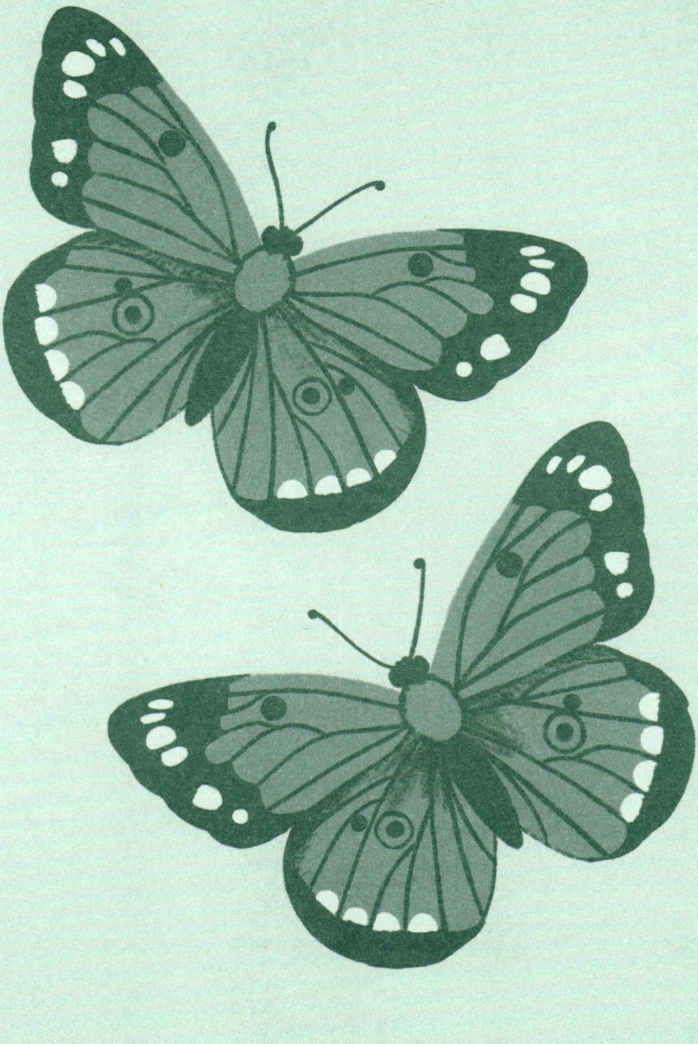

AUGUST

To Sit and Dream

1 AUGUST

XXXIII

FROM *TWASINTA'S SEMINOLES, OR THE RAPE OF FLORIDA*, CANTO I

'Come now, my love, the moon is on the lake;
Upon the waters is my light, canoe;
Come with me, love, and gladsome oars shall make
A music on the parting wave for you, –
Come o'er the waters deep and dark and blue
Come where the lilies in the marge have sprung,
Come with me, love, for Oh, my love is true!'
This is the song that on the lake was sung.
The boatman sang it over when his heart was young.

Albery Allson Whitman (1851–1901)

2 AUGUST

Marriage Morning

Light, so low upon earth,
   You send a flash to the sun.
Here is the golden close of love,
   All my wooing is done.
Oh, all the woods and the meadows,
   Woods, where we hid from the wet,
Stiles where we stayed to be kind,
   Meadows in which we met!
Light, so low in the vale
   You flash and lighten afar,
For this is the golden morning of love,
   And you are his morning star.
Flash, I am coming, I come,
   By meadow and stile and wood,
Oh, lighten into my eyes and my heart,
   Into my heart and my blood!
Heart, are you great enough
   For a love that never tires?
O heart, are you great enough for love?
   I have heard of thorns and briers.
Over the thorns and briers,
   Over the meadows and stiles,
Over the world to the end of it
   Flash of a million miles.

Alfred, Lord Tennyson (1809–1892)

3 AUGUST

Song

Oh, say not, my love, with that mortified air,
    That your spring-time of pleasure is flown,
Nor bid me to maids that are younger repair,
    For those raptures that still are thine own.

Though April his temples may wreathe with the vine,
    Its tendrils in infancy curl'd,
'Tis the ardour of August matures us the wine,
    Whose life-blood enlivens the world.

Though thy form that was fashion'd as light as a fay's,
    Has assumed a proportion more round,
And thy glance, that was bright as a falcon's at gaze,
    Looks soberly now on the ground, –

Enough, after absence to meet me again,
    Thy steps still with ecstasy move;
Enough, that those dear sober glances retain
    For me the kind language of love.

Sir Walter Scott (1771–1832)

4 AUGUST

In the Vaulted Way

In the vaulted way, where the passage turned
To the shadowy corner that none could see,
You paused for our parting, – plaintively:
Though overnight had come words that burned
My fond frail happiness out of me.

And then I kissed you, – despite my thought
That our spell must end when reflection came
On what you had deemed me, whose one long aim
Had been to serve you; that what I sought
Lay not in a heart that could breathe such blame.

But yet I kissed you: whereon you again
As of old kissed me. Why, why was it so?
Do you cleave to me after that light-tongued blow?
If you scorned me at eventide, how love then?
The thing is dark, Dear. I do not know.

Thomas Hardy (1840–1928)

5 AUGUST

Jour des Morts
(CIMITIÈRE MONTPARNASSE)

Sweetheart, is this the last of all our posies
   And little festivals, my flowers are they
But white and wistful ghosts of gayer roses
   Shut with you in this grim garden? Not to-day,
Ah! no! come out with me before the grey gate closes
   It is your fête and here is your bouquet!

Charlotte Mew (1869–1928)

6 AUGUST

Upon Julia's *Clothes*

When as in silks my *Julia* goes,
Then, then (me thinks) how sweetly flowes
That liquefaction of her clothes.

Next, when I cast mine eyes, and see
That brave Vibration each way free;
O how that glittering taketh me!

Robert Herrick (1591–1674)

7 AUGUST

A Life's Love

How I do love to sit and dream
   Of that sweet passion, when I meet
The lady I must love for life!
   The very thought makes my Soul beat
Its wings, as though it saw that light
Silver the rims of my black night.

I see her bring a crimson mouth
   To open at a kiss, and close;
I see her bring her two fair cheeks,
   That I may paint on each a rose;
I see her two hands, like doves white,
Fly into mine and hide from sight.

In fancy hear her soft, sweet voice;
   My eager Soul, to catch her words,
Waits at the ear, with Noah's haste
   To take God's message-bearing Birds;
What passion she will in me move –
That Lady I for life must love!

W. H. Davies (1871–1940)

8 AUGUST

Sonnet XL. Severed Selves

Two separate divided silences,
   Which, brought together, would find loving voice;
   Two glances which together would rejoice
In love, now lost like stars beyond dark trees;
Two hands apart whose touch alone gives ease;
   Two bosoms which, heart-shrined with mutual flame,
   Would, meeting in one clasp, be made the same;
Two souls, the shores wave-mocked of sundering seas:–

Such are we now. Ah! may our hope forecast
   Indeed one hour again, when on this stream
   Of darkened love once more the light shall gleam? –
An hour how slow to come, how quickly past, –
Which blooms and fades, and only leaves at last,
   Faint as shed flowers, the attenuated dream.

D. G. Rossetti (1828–1882)

9 AUGUST

For My Mother
(May I Inherit Half Her Strength)

LINES 1–16

My mother loved my father
I write this as an absolute
in this my thirtieth year
the year to discard absolutes

he appeared, her fate disguised,
as a sunday player in a cricket match,
he had ridden from a country
one hundred miles south of hers.

She tells me he dressed the part,
visiting dandy, maroon blazer,
cream serge pants, seam like razor
and the beret and the two-tone shoes.

My father stopped to speak to her sister,
till he looked and saw her by the oleander,
sure in the kingdom of my blue-eyed grandmother.
He never played the cricket match that day.

Lorna Goodison (b.1947)

10 AUGUST

Love's Philosophy

I

The fountains mingle with the river
   And the rivers with the Ocean,
The winds of Heaven mix for ever
   With a sweet emotion;
Nothing in the world is single;
   All things by a law divine
In one spirit meet and mingle.
   Why not I with thine? –

II

See the mountains kiss high Heaven
   And the waves clasp one another;
No sister-flower would be forgiven
   If it disdained its brother;
And the sunlight clasps the earth
   And the moonbeams kiss the sea:
What is all this sweet work worth
   If thou kiss not me?

Percy Bysshe Shelley (1792–1822)

11 AUGUST

He cannot deny Himself

Love still is Love, and doeth all things well,
Whether He show me heaven or hell,
   Or earth in her decay
   Passing away
   On a day.

Love still is Love, tho' He should say 'Depart,'
And break my incorrigible heart,
   And set me out of sight,
   Widowed of light
   In the night.

Love still is Love, is Love, if He should say,
'Come, 'on that uttermost dread day;
   'Come,' unto very me,
   'Come where I be,
   Come and see.'

Love still is Love, whatever comes to pass:
O Only Love, make me Thy glass,
   Thy pleasure to fulfil
   By loving still,
   Come what will.

Christina Rossetti (1830–1894)

12 AUGUST

A Subaltern's Love-song

Miss J. Hunter Dunn, Miss J. Hunter Dunn,
Furnish'd and burnish'd by Aldershot sun,
What strenuous singles we played after tea,
We in the tournament – you against me!

Love-thirty, love-forty, oh! weakness of joy,
The speed of a swallow, the grace of a boy,
With carefullest carelessness, gaily you won,
I am weak from your loveliness, Joan Hunter Dunn.

Miss Joan Hunter Dunn, Miss Joan Hunter Dunn,
How mad I am, sad I am, glad that you won,
The warm-handled racket is back in its press,
But my shock-headed victor, she loves me no less.

Her father's euonymus shines as we walk,
And swing past the summer-house, buried in talk,
And cool the verandah that welcomes us in
To the six-o'clock news and a lime juice and gin.

The scent of the conifers, sound of the bath,
The view from my bedroom of moss-dappled path,
As I struggle with double-end evening tie,
For we dance at the Golf Club, my victor and I.

On the floor of her bedroom lie blazer and shorts
And the cream-coloured walls are be-trophied with sports,
And westering, questioning settles the sun
On your low-leaded window, Miss Joan Hunter Dunn.

The Hillman is waiting, the light's in the hall,
The pictures of Egypt are bright on the wall,
My sweet, I am standing beside the oak stair
And there on the landing's the light on your hair.

By roads "not adopted", by woodlanded ways,
She drove to the club in the late summer haze,
Into nine-o'clock Camberley, heavy with bells
And mushroomy, pine-woody, evergreen smells.

Miss Joan Hunter Dunn, Miss Joan Hunter Dunn,
I can hear from the car-park the dance has begun.
Oh! full Surrey twilight! importunate band!
Oh! strongly adorable tennis-girl's hand.

Around us are Rovers and Austins afar,
Above us, the intimate roof of the car,
And here on my right is the girl of my choice,
With the tilt of her nose and the chime of her voice,

And the scent of her wrap, and the words never said,
And the ominous, ominous dancing ahead.
We sat in the car park till twenty to one
And now I'm engaged to Miss Joan Hunter Dunn.

John Betjeman (1906–1984)

13 AUGUST

Elegie: To His Mistress Going to Bed
LINES 1–18

Come, Madam, come, all rest my powers defie,
Until I labour, I in labour lie.
The foe oft-times having the foe in sight,
Is tir'd with standing though he never fight.
Off with that girdle, like heaven's Zone glistering,
But a far fairer world incompassing.
Unpin that spangled breastplate which you wear,
That th'eyes of busy fools may be stopt there.
Unlace your self, for that harmonious chyme,
Tells me from you, that now it is bed time.
Off with that happy busk, which I envie,
That still can be, and still can stand so nigh.
Your gown going off, such beauteous state reveals,
As when from flowry meads th'hills shadowe steales.
Off with that wyrie Coronet and shew
The haiery Diadem which on you doth grow:
Now off with those shoes, and then safely tread
In this loves hallow'd temple, this soft bed.

John Donne (1572–1631)

14 AUGUST

Love Song

Once in the world's first prime,
   When nothing lived or stirred,
Nothing but new-born Time,
   Nor was there even a bird –
The Silence spoke to a Star,
   But I do not dare repeat
What it said to its love afar:
   It was too sweet, too sweet.

But there, in the fair world's youth,
   Ere sorrow had drawn breath,
When nothing was known but Truth,
   Nor was there even death,
The Star to Silence was wed,
   And the Sun was priest that day,
And they made their bridal-bed
   High in the Milky Way.

For the great white star had heard
   Her silent lover's speech;
It needed no passionate word
   To pledge them each to each.
O lady fair and far,
   Hear, oh, hear, and apply!
Thou the beautiful Star –
   The voiceless Silence, I.

Ella Wheeler Wilcox (1850–1919)

15 AUGUST

Faintheart in a Railway Train

At nine in the morning there passed a church,
At ten there passed me by the sea,
At twelve a town of smoke and smirch,
At two a forest of oak and birch,
  And then, on a platform, she:

A radiant stranger, who saw not me.
I queried, 'Get out to her do I dare?'
But I kept my seat in my search for a plea,
And the wheels moved on. O could it but be
  That I had alighted there!

Thomas Hardy (1840–1928)

16 AUGUST

Girl in white

Don't think
because her petal thighs
leap and her slight
breasts flatten
against your chest
that you warm her
alligator mind.
In August
her hand of snow
rests on your back.
Follow her through the mirror.
My wan sister.
Love is a trap
that would tear her
like a rabbit.

Marge Piercy (b.1936)

17 AUGUST

Love guards the roses of thy lips

Love guards the roses of thy lips
   And flies about them like a bee;
If I approach he forward skips,
   And if I kiss he stingeth me.

Love in thine eyes doth build his bower,
   And sleeps within their pretty shine;
And if I look the boy will lower,
   And from their orbs shoot shafts divine.

Love works thy heart within his fire,
   And in my tears doth firm the same;
And if I tempt it will retire,
   And of my plaints doth make a game.

Love, let me cull her choicest flowers;
   And pity me, and calm her eye;
Make soft her heart, dissolve her lowers
   Then will I praise thy deity.

But if thou do not, Love, I'll truly serve her
In spite of thee, and by firm faith deserve her.

Thomas Lodge (1558–1625)

18 AUGUST

Give all to love

Give all to love;
Obey thy heart;
Friends, kindred, days,
Estate, good-fame,
Plans, credit and the Muse,–
Nothing refuse.

'Tis a brave master;
Let it have scope:
Follow it utterly,
Hope beyond hope:
High and more high
It dives into noon,
With wing unspent,
Untold intent:
But it is a god,
Knows its own path
And the outlets of the sky.

It was never for the mean;
It requireth courage stout.
Souls above doubt,
Valor unbending,
It will reward,–
They shall return
More than they were,
And ever ascending.

Leave all for love;
Yet, hear me, yet,
One word more thy heart behoved,
One pulse more of firm endeavor,–
Keep thee to-day,
To-morrow, forever,
Free as an Arab
Of thy beloved.

Cling with life to the maid;
But when the surprise,
First vague shadow of surmise
Flits across her bosom young,
Of a joy apart from thee,
Free be she, fancy-free;
Nor thou detain her vesture's hem,
Nor the palest rose she flung
From her summer diadem.

Though thou loved her as thyself,
As a self of purer clay,
Though her parting dims the day,
Stealing grace from all alive;
Heartily know,
When half-gods go,
The gods arrive.

Ralph Waldo Emerson (1803–1882)

19 AUGUST

XVIII

FROM *A SHROPSHIRE LAD*

Oh, when I was in love with you,
   Then I was clean and brave,
And miles around the wonder grew
   How well did I behave.

And now the fancy passes by,
   And nothing will remain,
And miles around they'll say that I
   Am quite myself again.

A. E. Housman (1859–1936)

20 AUGUST

A Love Fray

I will not love thee more,
   Be as it may.
Plead with me and implore,
   And say thy say,
I will not love thee more.

Yet smile, thou foolish one,
   Nor ask me why,
I could not love thee more
   Were I to try.

Willa Cather (1873–1947)

21 AUGUST

Modern Love

It is summer, and we are in a house
That is not ours, sitting at a table
Enjoying minutes of a rented silence,
The upstairs people gone. The pigeons lull
To sleep the under-tens and invalids,
The tree shakes out its shadows to the grass,
The roses rove through the wilds of my neglect.
Our lives flap, and we have no hope of better
Happiness than this, not much to show for love
But how we are, and how this evening is,
Unpeopled, silent, and where we are alive
In a domestic love, seemingly alone,
All other lives worn down to trees and sunlight,
Looking forward to a visit from the cat.

Douglas Dunn (b.1942)

22 AUGUST

The Passionate Shepherd to his Love

Come live with me and be my love,
And we will all the pleasures prove,
That hills and valleys, dales and fields,
And all the craggy mountains yields.

There we will sit upon the rocks,
And see the shepherds feed their flocks,
By shallow rivers to whose falls
Melodious birds sing madrigals.

And I will make thee beds of roses
With a thousand fragrant posies,
A cap of flowers, and a kirtle,
Embroidered all with leaves of myrtle;

A gown made of the finest wool
Which from our pretty lambs we pull;
Fair lined slippers for the cold,
With buckles of the purest gold;

A belt of straw and ivy-buds,
With coral clasps and amber studs:
And if these pleasures may thee move,
Come live with me and be my love.

The shepherds' swains shall dance and sing
For thy delight each May morning:
If these delights thy mind may move,
Then live with me and be my love.

Christopher Marlowe (1564–1593)

23 AUGUST

The Nimphs Reply to the Sheepheard

If all the world and love were young,
And truth in every Sheepheards tongue,
These pretty pleasures might me move,
To live with thee, and be thy love.

Time drives the flocks from field to fold,
When Rivers rage and Rocks grow cold,
And Philomell becommeth dombe,
The rest complaines of cares to come.

The flowers doe fade, and wanton fieldes,
To wayward winter reckoning yeelds,
A honny tongue, a hart of gall,
Is fancies spring, but sorrowes fall.

Thy gownes, thy shoes, thy beds of Roses,
Thy cap, thy kirtle, and thy posies
Soone breake, soone wither, soone forgotten:
In follie ripe, in reason rotten.

Thy belt of straw and Ivie buddes,
The Corall claspes and Amber studdes,
All these in mee no meanes can move
To come to thee and be thy love.

But could youth last, and love still breede,
Had joyes no date, nor age no neede,
Then these delights my minde might move
To live with thee, and be thy love.

Sir Walter Raleigh (c.1552–1618)

24 AUGUST

I looked here

FROM *THE BLACK RIDERS*

I looked here.
I looked there.
Nowhere could I see my love.
And – this time –
She was in my heart.
Truly, then, I have no complaint,
For though she be fair and fairer,
She is none so fair as she
In my heart.

Stephen Crane (1871–1900)

25 AUGUST

As Chloris full of harmless thought

As Cloris full of harmless thought,
   Beneath the willows lay,
Kind love a comely shepherd brought
   To pass the time away.
She blushed to be encountered so,
   And chid the amorous swain;
But as she strove to rise and go,
   He pulled her down again.

A sudden passion seized her heart,
   In spite of her disdain,
She found a pulse in every part,
   And love in every vein:
'Ah, youth,' quoth she, 'what charms are these,
   That conquer and surprise?
Ah let me, for unless you please,
   I have no power to rise.'

She faintly spoke, and trembling lay,
   For fear he should comply,
But virgins' eyes their hearts betray,
   And give their tongues the lie.
Thus she who princes had denied,
   With all their pompous train,
Was in the lucky minute tried,
   And yielded to a swain.

John Wilmot, Lord Rochester (1647–1680)

26 AUGUST

A True Maid

'No, no; for my virginity,
   When I lose that,' says Rose, 'I'll die':
'Behind the elms, last night,' cried Dick,
   'Rose, were you not extremely sick?'

Matthew Prior (1664–1721)

27 AUGUST

The Ring

FROM *THE MARRIAGE OF PSYCHE*

He has married me with a ring, a ring of bright water
Whose ripples travel from the heart of the sea,
He has married me with a ring of light, the glitter
Broadcast on the swift river.
He has married me with the sun's circle
Too dazzling to see, traced in summer sky.
He has crowned me with the wreath of white cloud
That gathers on the snowy summit of the mountain,
Ringed me round with the world-circling wind,
Bound me to the whirlwind's centre.
He has married me with the orbit of the moon
And with the boundless circle of the stars,
With the orbits that measure years, months, days and nights,
Set the tides flowing,
Command the winds to travel or be at rest.

At the ring's centre,
Spirit or angel troubling the still pool,
Causality not in nature,
Finger's touch that summons at a point, a moment
Stars and planets, life and light
Or gathers cloud about an apex of cold,
Transcendent touch of love summons world to being.

Kathleen Raine (1908–2003)

28 AUGUST

My delight and thy delight

My delight and thy delight
Walking, like two angels white,
In the gardens of the night:

My desire and thy desire
Twining to a tongue of fire,
Leaping live, and laughing higher;
Thro' the everlasting strife
In the mystery of life.

Love, from whom the world begun,
Hath the secret of the sun.

Love can tell, and love alone,
Whence the million stars were strewn,
Why each atom knows its own,
How, in spite of woe and death,
Gay is life, and sweet is breath:

This he taught us, this we knew,
Happy in his science true,
Hand in hand as we stood
Neath the shadows of the wood,
Heart to heart as we lay
In the dawning of the day.

Robert Bridges (1844–1930)

29 AUGUST

Love III

Love bade me welcome. Yet my soul drew back
        Guilty of dust and sin.
But quick-ey'd Love, observing me grow slack
        From my first entrance in,
Drew nearer to me, sweetly questioning,
        If I lack'd any thing.

A guest, I answer'd, worthy to be here:
        Love said, You shall be he.
I the unkind, ungrateful? Ah my dear,
        I cannot look on thee.
Love took my hand, and smiling did reply,
        Who made the eyes but I?

Truth Lord, but I have marr'd them: let my shame
        Go where it doth deserve.
And know you not, says Love, who bore the blame?
        My dear, then I will serve.
You must sit down, says Love, and taste my meat:
        So I did sit and eat.

George Herbert (1593–1633)

30 AUGUST

To M. E. A.

Oh! had I that poetic lore
  Bestowed upon the favored few,
To ope' Dame Nature's bounteous store,
  And hold her treasures up to view,
To climb Parnassus' lofty mount,
Or taste the Muses' sacred fount,
The far-famed Heliconian spring,
Which Grecian poets erst did sing, –
And did Apollo, and the Nine,
With eloquence and verse divine,
Direct my pen – I scarce could tell
The numerous charms which in thee dwell.
Thy loveliness of form and face
Might serve as model for a Grace;
And the bright luster of thine eye
Mahomet's Houris far outvie.
The nobler beauties of the mind,
  Refined and elevated taste;
Great moral purity, combined
  With every outward charm and grace
And reason, governing the whole,
Displays in every act, a soul
High raised above the things which bind
Down to the earth more sordid minds;
And, soaring fetterless and free
In its unsullied purity,
Seems like a seraph wandering here,
The native of a brighter sphere.

James Monroe Whitfield (1822–1871)

31 AUGUST

Tuscan Olives III

We climbed one morning to the sunny height
   Where chestnuts grow no more and olives grow;
Far-off the circling mountains cinder-white,
   The yellow river and the gorge below.

'Turn round,' you said, O flower of Paradise;
   I did not turn, I looked upon your eyes.
'Turn round,' you said, 'turn round and see the view!'
   I did not turn, my Love, I looked at you.

A. Mary F. Robinson (1857–1944)

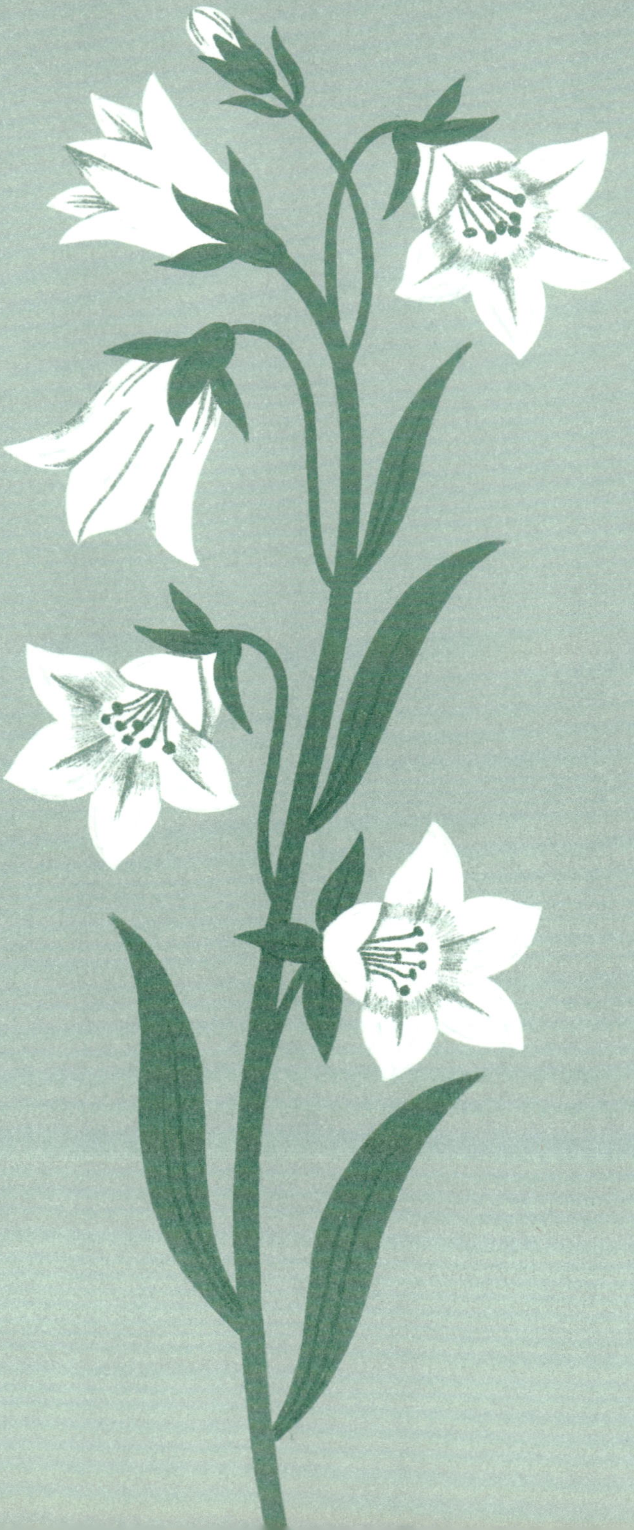

SEPTEMBER

A Thrill in My Heart

1 SEPTEMBER

Sonnet 130

My mistress' eyes are nothing like the sun;
Coral is far more red than her lips' red;
If snow be white, why then her breasts are dun;
If hairs be wires, black wires grow on her head.
I have seen roses damasked, red and white,
But no such roses see I in her cheeks;
And in some perfumes is there more delight
Than in the breath that from my mistress reeks.
I love to hear her speak, yet well I know
That music hath a far more pleasing sound;
I grant I never saw a goddess go;
My mistress when she walks treads on the ground.
   And yet, by heaven, I think my love as rare
   As any she belied with false compare.

William Shakespeare (1564–1616)

2 SEPTEMBER

A September Night

The full September moon sheds floods of light,
And all the bayou's face is gemmed with stars,
Save where are dropped fantastic shadows down
From sycamores and moss-hung cypress trees.
With slumberous sound the waters half asleep
Creep on and on their way, twixt rankish reeds,
Through marsh and lowlands stretching to the gulf.
Begirt with cotton fields, Anguilla sits
Half bird-like, dreaming on her summer nest.
Amid her spreading figs and roses, still
In bloom with all their spring and summer hues,
Pomegranates hang with dapple cheeks full ripe,
And over all the town a dreamy haze
Drops down. The great plantations, stretching far
Away, are plains of cotton, downy white.
O, glorious is this night of joyous sounds;
Too full for sleep. Aromas wild and sweet,
From muscadine, late blooming jessamine,
And roses, all the heavy air suffuse.
Faint bellows from the alligators come
From swamps afar, where sluggish lagoons give
To them a peaceful home. The katydids
Make ceaseless cries. Ten thousand insects' wings
Stir in the moonlight haze and joyous shouts
Of Negro song and mirth awake hard by
The cabin dance. O, glorious is this night!
The Summer sweetness fills my heart with songs,
I can not sing, with loves I can not speak.

George Marion McClellan (1860–1934)

3 SEPTEMBER

Lullaby

Lay your sleeping head, my love,
Human on my faithless arm;
Time and fevers burn away
Individual beauty from
Thoughtful children, and the grave
Proves the child ephemeral:
But in my arms till break of day
Let the living creature lie,
Mortal, guilty, but to me
The entirely beautiful.

Soul and body have no bounds:
To lovers as they lie upon
Her tolerant enchanted slope
In their ordinary swoon,
Grave the vision Venus sends
Of supernatural sympathy,
Universal love and hope;
While an abstract insight wakes
Among the glaciers and the rocks
The hermit's carnal ecstasy.

Certainty, fidelity
On the stroke of midnight pass
Like vibrations of a bell,
And fashionable madmen raise
Their pedantic boring cry:
Every farthing of the cost,
All the dreaded cards foretell,
Shall be paid, but from this night
Not a whisper, not a thought,
Not a kiss nor look be lost.

Beauty, midnight, vision dies:
Let the winds of dawn that blow
Softly round your dreaming head
Such a day of welcome show
Eye and knocking heart may bless,
Find the mortal world enough;
Noons of dryness find you fed
By the involuntary powers,
Nights of insult let you pass
Watched by every human love.

W. H. Auden (1907–1973)

4 SEPTEMBER

Song. Sudden Light

I have been here before,
    But when or how I cannot tell:
I know the grass beyond the door,
    The sweet keen smell,
The sighing sound, the lights around the shore.

You have been mine before,–
    How long ago I may not know:
But just when at that swallow's soar
    Your neck turned so,
Some veil did fall, – I knew it all of yore.

Then now, – perchance again! . . .
    O round mine eyes your tresses shake!
Shall we not lie as we have lain
    Thus for Love's sake,
And sleep, and wake, yet never break the chain?

D. G. Rossetti (1828–1882)

5 SEPTEMBER

When as the rye reach to the chin

When as the rye reach to the chin,
   And chopcherry, chopcherry ripe within,
Strawberries swimming in the cream,
And school-boys played in the stream;
   Then O, then O, then O my true love said,
     Till that time come again,
   She could not live a maid.

George Peele (1556–1596)

6 SEPTEMBER

A Thunderstorm in Town

(A REMINISCENCE: 1893)

She wore a 'terra-cotta' dress,
And we stayed, because of the pelting storm,
Within the hansom's dry recess,
Though the horse had stopped; yea, motionless
   We sat on, snug and warm.

Then the downpour ceased, to my sharp sad pain,
And the glass that had screened our forms before
Flew up, and out she sprang to her door:
I should have kissed her if the rain
   Had lasted a minute more.

Thomas Hardy (1840–1928)

7 SEPTEMBER

The Charming Woman

So Miss Myrtle is going to marry?
   What a number of hearts she will break!
There's Lord George, and Tom Brown, and Sir Harry,
   Who are dying of love for her sake!
'Tis a match that we all must approve, –
   Let gossips say all that they can!
For indeed she's a charming woman,
   And he's a most fortunate man!

Yes, indeed, she's a charming woman,
   And she reads both Latin and Greek,–
And I'm told that she solved a problem
   In Euclid before she could speak!
Had she been but a daughter of mine,
   I'd have taught her to hem and to sew, –
But her mother (a charming woman)
   Couldn't think of such trifles, you know!

Oh, she's really a charming woman!
   But, perhaps, a little too thin;
And no wonder such very late hours
   Should ruin her beautiful skin!
And her shoulders are rather too bare.
   And her gown's nearly up to her knees,
But I'm told that these charming women
   May dress themselves just as they please!

Yes, she's really a charming woman!
   But, I thought, I observed, by the bye,
A something – that's rather uncommon, –
   In the flash of that very bright eye?
It may be a mere fancy of mine,
   Tho' her voice has a very sharp tone, –
But I'm told that these charming women
   Are inclined to have wills of their own!

She sings like a bullfinch or linnet,
   And she talks like an Archbishop too;
Can play you a rubber and win it, –
   If she's got nothing better to do!
She can chatter of Poor-laws and Tithes,
   And the value of labour and land,–
'Tis a pity when charming women
   Talk of things which they don't understand.

I'm told that she hasn't a penny.
   Yet her gowns would make Maradan stare;
And I feel her bills must be many, –
   But that's only her husband's affair!
Such husbands are very uncommon,
   So regardless of prudence and pelf, –
But they say such a charming woman
   Is a fortune, you know, in herself!

She's brothers and sisters by dozens.
   And all charming people, they say!
And several tall Irish cousins.
   Whom she loves in a sisterly way.
O young men, if you'd take my advice,
   You would find it an excellent plan, –
Don't marry a charming woman.
   If you are a sensible man!

Helen, Lady Dufferin (1807–1867)

8 SEPTEMBER

Sir William Dyer

MONUMENT TO SIR WILLIAM DYER, ERECTED BY HIS WIFE IN 1641,
ST. DENYS CHURCH, COLMWORTH

If a large hart, joynd with a noble mind
Shewing true worth, unto all good inclind
If faith in friendship, justice unto all,
Leave such a memory as we may call
Happy, thine is; then pious marble keepe
His just fame waking, though his lov'd dust sleepe.
And though death can devoure all that hath breath,
And monuments them selves have had a death,
Nature shan't suffer this, to ruinate,
Nor time demolish't, nor an envious fate,
Rais'd by just a hand, not vaine glorious pride,
Who'd be conceal'd, wer't modesty to hide
Such an affection did so long survive
The object of't; yet lov'd it as alive.
And this greate blessing to his name doth give
To make it by his tombe, and issue live.

My dearest dust could not thy hasty day
Afford thy drowzy patience leave to stay
One hower longer: so that wee might either
Sate up, or gone to bedd together?
But since thy finisht labor hath possessed
Thy weary limbs with early rest,
Enjoy it sweetly; and thy widdowe bride
Shall soone repose her by thy slumbring side;
Whose business, now, is only to prepare
My nightly dress, and call to prayer:
Mine eyes wax heavy and the day grows old.
The dew falls thick, my bloud grows cold.
Draw, draw the closed curtaynes: and make room:
My deare, my dearest dust; I come, I come.

Katherine, Lady Dyer (c.1585–1654)

9 SEPTEMBER

Shepherdess

All day my sheep have mingled with yours. They strayed
Into your valley seeking a change of ground.
Held and bemused with what they and I had found,
Pastures and wonders, heedlessly I delayed.

Now it is late. The tracks leading home are steep.
The stars and landmarks in your country are strange.
How can I take my sheep back over the range?
Shepherdess, show me now where I may sleep.

Norman Cameron (1905–1953)

10 SEPTEMBER

Song: To Lucasta, Going beyond the Seas
FROM LUCASTA

If to be absent were to be
    Away from thee;
  Or that when I am gone
  You or I were alone;
  Then, my Lucasta, might I crave
Pity from blustering wind or swallowing wave.

  But I'll not sigh one blast or gale
    To swell my sail,
  Or pay a tear to assuage
  The foaming blue god's rage;
  For whether he will let me pass
Or no, I'm still as happy as I was.

Though seas and land betwixt us both,
    Our faith and troth,
  Like separated souls,
  All time and space controls:
  Above the highest sphere we meet
Unseen, unknown; and greet as angels greet.

  So then we do anticipate
    Our after-fate,
  And are alive i' th' skies,
  If thus our lips and eyes
  Can speak like spirits unconfined
In heaven, their earthy bodies left behind.

Richard Lovelace (1617–1657)

11 SEPTEMBER

Talking in Bed

Talking in bed ought to be easiest,
Lying together there goes back so far,
An emblem of two people being honest.

Yet more and more time passes silently.
Outside, the wind's incomplete unrest
Builds and disperses clouds in the sky,

And dark towns heap up on the horizon.
None of this cares for us. Nothing shows why
At this unique distance from isolation

It becomes still more difficult to find
Words at once true and kind,
Or not untrue and not unkind.

Philip Larkin (1922–1985)

12 SEPTEMBER

The Shepherd's Wife's Song

Ah! what is love? It is a pretty thing,
As sweet unto a shepherd as a king,
   And sweeter too;
For kings have cares that wait upon a crown,
And cares can make the sweetest love to frown.
   Ah then, ah then,
If country loves such sweet desires gain,
What lady would not love a shepherd swain?

His flocks are folded, he comes home a night,
As merry as a king in his delight,
   And merrier too;
For kings bethink them what the state require,
Where shepherds careless carol by the fire.
   Ah then, ah then,
If country loves such sweet desires gain,
What lady would not love a shepherd swain?

He kisseth first, then sits as blithe to eat
His cream and curds, as doth the king his meat,
   And blither too;
For kings have often fears when they do sup,
Where shepherds dread no poison in their cup.
   Ah then, ah then,
If country loves such sweet desires gain,
What lady would not love a shepherd swain?

To bed he goes, as wanton then I ween,
As is a king in dalliance with a queen,
   More wanton too;
For kings have many griefs affects to move,
Where shepherds have no greater grief than love.
   Ah then, ah then,
If country loves such sweet desires gain,
What lady would not love a shepherd swain?

Upon his couch of straw he sleeps as sound,
As doth the king upon his bed of down,
   More sounder too;
For cares cause kings full oft their sleep to spill,
Where weary shepherds lie and snort their fill.
   Ah then, ah then,
If country loves such sweet desires gain,
What lady would not love a shepherd swain?

Thus with his wife he spends the year as blithe,
As doth king at every tide or sithe,
   And blither too;
For kings have war and broils to take in hand,
Where shepherds laugh, and love upon the land.
   Ah then, ah then,
If country loves such sweet desires gain,
What lady would not love a shepherd swain?

Robert Greene (1558–1592)

13 SEPTEMBER

So, We'll Go No More a Roving

I

So, we'll go no more a roving
    So late into the night,
Though the heart be still as loving,
    And the moon be still as bright.

II

For the sword outwears its sheath,
    And the soul outwears the breast,
And the heart must pause to breathe,
    And love itself have rest.

III

Though the night was made for loving,
    And the day returns too soon,
Yet we'll go no more a roving
    By the light of the moon.

Lord George Gordon Byron (1788–1824)

14 SEPTEMBER

Love is Enough: The Music

Love is enough: though the World be a-waning,
And the woods have no voice but the voice of complaining,
   Though the sky be too dark for dim eyes to discover
The gold-cups and daisies fair blooming thereunder,
Though the hills be held shadows, and the sea a dark wonder
   And this day draw a veil over all deeds passed over,
Yet their hands shall not tremble, their feet shall not falter;
The void shall not weary, the fear shall not alter
   These lips and these eyes of the loved and the lover.

William Morris (1834–1896)

15 SEPTEMBER

Song

How pleasant is love
When forbid or unknown;
Was my passion approved,
It would quickly be gone.

It adds to the charms,
When we steal the delight;
Why should love be exposed
Since himself has no sight?

In some sylvan shade
Let me sigh for my swain,
Where none but an echo
Will speak on't again.

Thus silent and soft
I'll pass the time on,
And when I grow weary,
I'll make my love known.

Sarah Fyge Egerton (c.1670–c.1723)

16 SEPTEMBER

Ruth

She stood breast high amid the corn,
Clasp'd by the golden light of morn,
Like the sweetheart of the sun,
Who many a glowing kiss had won.

On her cheek an autumn flush,
Deeply ripened;– such a blush
In the midst of brown was born,
Like red poppies grown with corn.

Round her eyes her tresses fell,
Which were blackest none could tell,
But long lashes veil'd a light,
That had else been all too bright.

And her hat, with shady brim,
Made her tressy forehead dim;–
Thus she stood amid the stooks,
Praising God with sweetest looks:–

Sure, I said, heav'n did not mean,
Where I reap thou shouldst but glean,
Lay thy sheaf adown and come,
Share my harvest and my home.

Thomas Hood (1799–1845)

17 SEPTEMBER

Love in Mayfair

I must tell you, my dear,
    I'm in love with him vastly!
Twenty thousand a year,
I must tell you, my dear!
He will soon be a peer –
    And such diamonds! – and, lastly
I must tell you, my dear,
    I'm in love with him vastly!

May Probyn (1856–1909)

18 SEPTEMBER

To lose thee

To lose thee – sweeter than to gain
All other hearts I knew.
'Tis true the drought is destitute,
But then, I had the dew!

The Caspian has its realms of sand,
Its other realm of sea.
Without the sterile perquisite,
No Caspian could be.

Emily Dickinson (1830–1886)

19 SEPTEMBER

On Love

FROM *THE PROPHET*

When love beckons to you, follow him.
Though his ways are hard and steep.
And when his wings enfold you yield to him.
Though the sword hidden among his pinions may wound you.
And when he speaks to you believe in him.
Though his voice may shatter your dreams as the north
  wind lays waste the garden.
......
For even as love crowns you so shall he crucify you.
  Even as he is for your growth so is he
    for your pruning.
Even as he ascends to your height and caresses your
tenderest branches that quiver in the sun,
So shall he descend to your roots and shake them in their
  clinging to the earth.
Like sheaves of corn he gathers you unto himself.
He threshes you to make you naked.
He sifts you to free you from your husks.
He grinds you to whiteness.
He kneads you until you are pliant;
And then he assigns you to his sacred fire, that you may
  become sacred bread for God's
    sacred feast.

All these things shall love do unto you that you may know
  the secrets of your heart, and in
    that knowledge become a fragment of Life's heart.

Kahlil Gibran (1883–1931)

20 SEPTEMBER

Fragment

This love of nature, that allures to take
Irregularity for harmony
Of larger scope than our hard measures make,
Cherish it as thy school for when on thee
The ills of life descend.

George Meredith (1828–1909)

21 SEPTEMBER

Eye of the Beholder

Learn to know
That beauty which, though aging,
Never will grow old:
Every line, a story, told;
Every wrinkle, a memory, etched;
Each dimple, a well from which
Laughter is drawn.

To have compassion, too –
Yes, even for the furrowed brow,
Which bears the marks
Of crosses, borne;
And fondness, for the scars
Of courage met and mettle, shown
In battles lost, or won;
And duels, fought at dawn
For you.

Petals, unfolding;
Passion, holding.
Nectar, ever sweeter
Towards the centre.

May such a beauty,
In all its layers,
From youth to maturity,
And such a love,
Be ours, for eternity.

Jana Synková (b.1968)

22 SEPTEMBER

Anacreon

The Muses found young Love one day,
    When mamma was not there,
They bound and carried him away
    To serve the Graces fair.
When Aphrodite found him gone,
    She thought him rather young,
And wrathfully she hastened on
    To free her captive son.
But when she cut the bonds of fate
    Ah! Sad the tale to tell,
The laddie's mamma came too late
    He liked his job too well.

Willa Cather (1873–1947)

23 SEPTEMBER

Pōkarekare Ana

TRADITIONAL MAORI SONG

They are agitated
the waters of Waiapu,
If you cross over girl
they will be calm.

Oh girl
return to me,
I could die
of love for you.

I've written my letter
I've sent my ring,
so that your people can see I'm troubled.

My pen is shattered,
I have no more paper
But my love
is still steadfast.

Never will my love
be dried by the sun,
It will be moistened
by my tears.

arranged by **Paraire 'Friday' Henare Tomoana (1874/5–1946)**

24 SEPTEMBER

My bounty is as boundless as the sea
FROM *ROMEO AND JULIET*, ACT II, SCENE II

Juliet:
My bounty is as boundless as the sea,
My love as deep: the more I give to thee
The more I have, for both are infinite.

William Shakespeare (1564–1616)

25 SEPTEMBER

Her Thought and His

The gray of the sea, and the gray of the sky,
A glimpse of the moon like a half-closed eye.
The gleam on the waves and the light on the land,
A thrill in my heart, – and – my sweetheart's hand.

She turned from the sea with a woman's grace,
And the light fell soft on her upturned face,
And I thought of the flood-tide of infinite bliss
That would flow to my heart from a single kiss.

But my sweetheart was shy, so I dared not ask
For the boon, so bravely I wore the mask.
But into her face there came a flame:–
I wonder could she have been thinking the same?

Paul Laurence Dunbar (1872–1906)

26 SEPTEMBER

Song

A Scholar first my Love implor'd,
And then an empty titled Lord;
The Pedant, talk'd in lofty Strains;
Alas! his Lordship wanted Brains:
I list'ned not, to one or t'other,
But strait referr'd them to my Mother.

A Poet next my Love assail'd,
A Lawyer hop'd to have prevail'd;
The Bard too much approv'd himself,
The Lawyer thirsted after Pelf:
I list'ned not, to one or t'other,
But still referr'd them to my Mother.

An Officer, my Heart wou'd storm,
A Miser, sought me too, in Form;
But *Mars*, was over-free and bold,
The Miser's Heart was in his Gold:
I list'ned not, to one or t'other,
Referring still unto my Mother.

And after them, some twenty more,
Successless were, as those before;
When *Damon*, lovely *Damon*, came,
Our Hearts strait felt a mutual Flame:
I vow'd I'd have him, and no other,
Without referring, to my Mother.

Lady Dorothy Dubois (1728–1774)

27 SEPTEMBER

To a Lady on Her Passion for Old China

LINES 1–10

What ecstasies her bosom fire!
How her eyes languish with desire!
How blest, how happy should I be,
Were that fond glance bestow'd on me!
New doubts and fears within me war:
What rival's near? a china jar.

    China's the passion of her soul;
A cup, a plate, a dish, a bowl,
Can kindle wishes in her breast,
Inflame with joy, or break her rest.

John Gay (1685–1732)

28 SEPTEMBER

Mixed Marriages

Mixed marriages do have their advantages.
We express our needs and tiffs in two languages.

John Agard (b.1949)

29 SEPTEMBER

An Evening Song

   Good night, love!
May heaven's brightest stars watch over thee!
Good angels spread their wings, and cover thee;
    And through the night,
      So dark and still,
    Spirits of light
      Charm thee from ill!
My heart is hovering round thy dwelling-place,
Good night, dear love! God bless thee with his grace!

   Good night, love!
Soft lullabies the night-wind sing to thee!
And on its wings sweet odours bring to thee;
    And in thy dreaming
      May all things dear,
    With gentle seeming,
      Come smiling near!
My knees are bowed, my hands are clasped in prayer –
Good night, dear love! God keep thee in his care!

Frances Anne Kemble (1809–1893)

30 SEPTEMBER

Celia, Celia

When I am sad and weary
When I think all hope has gone
When I walk along High Holborn
I think of you with nothing on.

Adrian Mitchell (1932–2008)

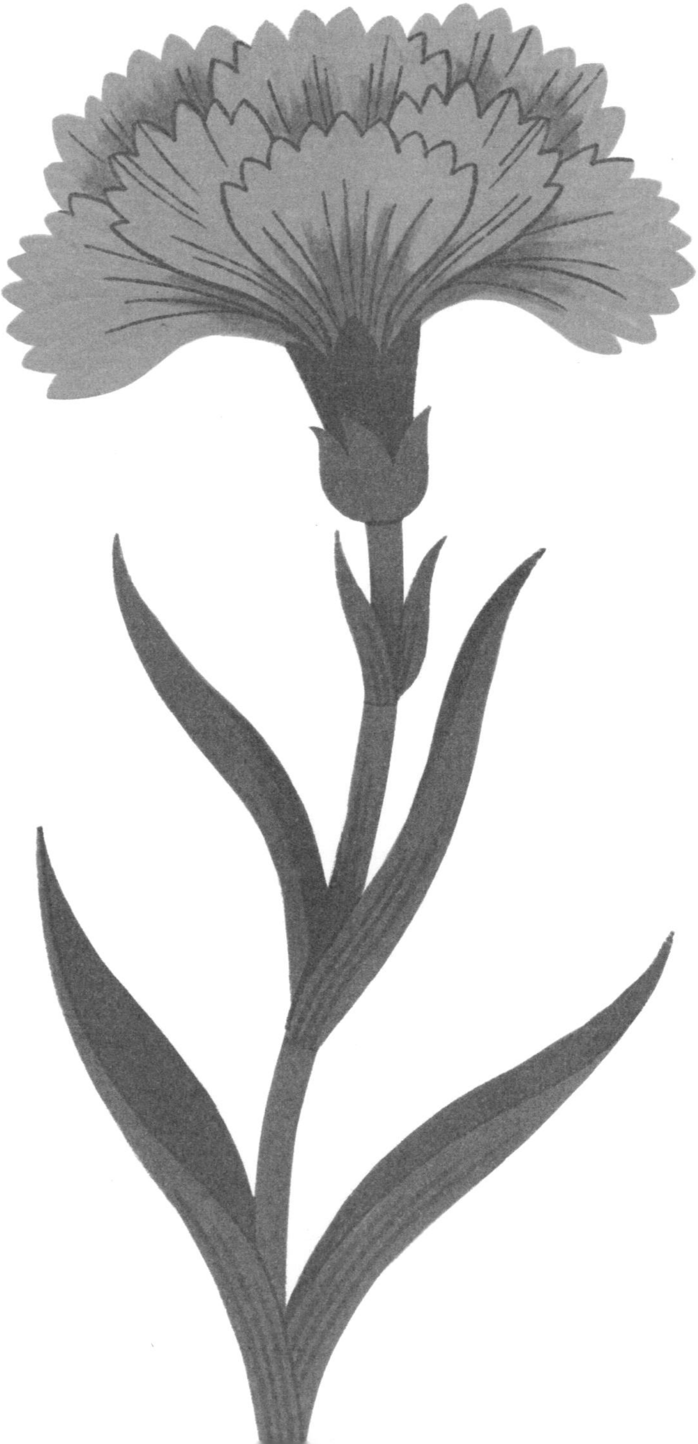

OCTOBER

Gathered to Thy Heart

1 OCTOBER

Verses Written in a Garden

See how the pair of billing doves
With open murmurs own their loves;
And, heedless of censorious eyes,
Pursue their unpolluted joys;
No fears of future want molest
The downy quiet of their nest:
No interest joined the happy pair,
Securely blest in Nature's care,
While her dictates they pursue;
For constancy is Nature too.
   Can all the doctrine of the schools,
Our maxims, our religious rules,
Can learning to our lives ensure,
Virtue so bright, or bliss so pure?
The great Creator's happy ends,
Virtue and pleasure ever blends:
In vain the church and court have tried
Th' united essence to divide;
Alike they find their wild mistake,
The pedant priest, and giddy rake.

Lady Mary Wortley Montagu (1689–1762)

2 OCTOBER

Sonnet

WRITTEN ON A BLANK PAGE IN SHAKESPEARE'S POEMS,
FACING 'A LOVER'S COMPLAINT'.

Bright star, would I were stedfast as thou art—
    Not in lone splendour hung aloft the night
And watching, with eternal lids apart,
    Like nature's patient, sleepless Eremite,
The moving waters at their priestlike task
    Of pure ablution round earth's human shores,
Or gazing on the new soft-fallen mask
    Of snow upon the mountains and the moors—
No—yet still stedfast, still unchangeable,
    Pillow'd upon my fair love's ripening breast,
To feel for ever its soft fall and swell,
    Awake for ever in a sweet unrest,
Still, still to hear her tender-taken breath,
    And so live ever—or else swoon to death.

John Keats (1795–1821)

3 OCTOBER

Love

Love is a wild wonder
And stars that sing,
Rocks that burst asunder
And mountains that take wing.

John Henry with his hammer
Makes a little spark.
That little spark is love
Dying in the dark.

Langston Hughes (1901–1967)

4 OCTOBER

The Ragged Wood

O hurry where by water among the trees
The delicate-stepping stag and his lady sigh,
When they have but looked upon their images –
Would none had ever loved but you and I!

Or have you heard that sliding silver-shoed
Pale silver-proud queen-woman of the sky,
When the sun looked out of his golden hood? –
O that none ever loved but you and I!

O hurry to the ragged wood, for there
I will drive all those lovers out and cry –
O my share of the world, O yellow hair!
No one has ever loved but you and I.

W. B. Yeats (1865–1939)

5 OCTOBER

Song: Eternity of Love Protested

How ill doth he deserve a lover's name,
                Whose pale weak flame
                Cannot retain
His heat, in spite of absence or disdain,
But doth at once, like paper set on fire,
                Burn, and expire!
True love can never change his seat,
Nor did her ever love, that could retreat.

That noble flame which my breast keeps alive
                Shall still survive
                When my soul's fled;
Nor shall my love die when my body's dead,
That shall wait on me to the lower shade,
                And never fade;
My very ashes in their urn
Shall, like a hallow'd lamp, forever burn.

Thomas Carew (1595–1640)

6 OCTOBER

At the Wedding March

God with honour hang your head,
Groom, and grace you, bride, your bed
With lissome scions, sweet scions,
Out of hallowed bodies bred.

Each be other's comfort kind:
Déep, déeper than divined,
Divine charity, dear charity,
Fast you ever, fast bind.

Then let the March tread our ears:
I to him turn with tears
Who to wedlock, his wonder wedlock,
Déals tríumph and immortal years.

Gerard Manley Hopkins (1844–1889)

7 OCTOBER

A Match

If love were what the rose is,
   And I were like the leaf,
Our lives would grow together
In sad or singing weather,
Blown fields or flowerful closes,
   Green pasture or grey grief;
If love were what the rose is,
   And I were like the leaf.

If I were what the words are,
   And love were like the tune,
With double sound and single
Delight our lips would mingle,
With kisses glad as birds are
   That get sweet rain at noon;
If I were what the words are,
   And love were like the tune.

If you were life, my darling,
   And I your love were death,
We'd shine and snow together
Ere March made sweet the weather
With daffodil and starling
   And hours of fruitful breath;
If you were life, my darling,
   And I your love were death.

If you were thrall to sorrow,
   And I were page to joy,
We'd play for lives and seasons
With loving looks and treasons
And tears of night and morrow
   And laughs of maid and boy;
If you were thrall to sorrow,
   And I were page to joy.

If you were April's lady,
   And I were lord in May,
We'd throw with leaves for hours
And draw for days with flowers,
Till day like night were shady
   And night were bright like day;
If you were April's lady,
   And I were lord in May.

If you were queen of pleasure,
   And I were king of pain,
We'd hunt down love together,
Pluck out his flying-feather,
And teach his feet a measure,
   And find his mouth a rein;
If you were queen of pleasure,
   And I were king of pain.

Algernon Charles Swinburne (1837–1909)

8 OCTOBER

Two Lips

I kissed them in fancy as I came
   Away in the morning glow:
I kissed them through the glass of her picture-frame:
    She did not know.

I kissed them in love, in troth, in laughter,
   When she knew all; long so!
That I should kiss them in a shroud thereafter
    She did not know.

Thomas Hardy (1840–1928)

9 OCTOBER

Sonnet

Leave me, O Love, which reachest but to dust,
And thou, my mind, aspire to higher things;
Grow rich in that which never taketh rust;
Whatever fades but fading pleasure brings.
Draw in thy beams and humble all thy might
To that sweet yoke where lasting freedoms be;
Which breaks the clouds and opens forth the light,
That doth both shine and give us sight to see.
O take fast hold; let that light be thy guide
In this small course which birth draws out to death,
And think how evil becometh him to slide,
Who seeketh heaven, and comes of heavenly breath.
   Then farewell, world; thy uttermost I see:
   Eternal Love, maintain thy life in me.

Splendidis longum valedico nugis

Sir Philip Sidney (1554–1586)

10 OCTOBER

An Ode Composed in Sleep

Lovely fairy! Charming sprite!
   Kindly listen and appear,
Whether bathed in dewdrops bright,
   Or in chrystal riv'lets clear.

Howe'er divine, the mortal youth
   Yet hopes thy gentleness to move,
With the soft energy of truth,
   And the prevailing voice of love.

Judith Madan (1702–1781)

11 OCTOBER

Wishes to his (Supposed) Mistress
VERSES 1–5

Whoe'er she be,
That not impossible she
That shall command my heart and me;

Where'er she lie,
Locked up from mortal eye
In shady leaves of destiny

Till that ripe birth
Of studied fate stand forth,
And teach her fair steps to our Earth;

Till that divine
Idea take a shrine
Of crystal flesh, through which to shine;

Meet you her, my wishes,
Bespeak her to my blisses,
And be ye called my absent kisses.

Richard Crashaw (1612–1649)

12 OCTOBER

The Caveman's Lament

me think about her when sun rises
me think about her when sun sets
me say to her how much me love her
she tell me love invent not yet

me make cave all warm and cosy
me lie bearskin on cave floor
me play song of love on bone flute
she choose cave of Tim next door

me no more go out hunt mammoth
me throw spear too short or long
me sit in cave paint her picture
she say me got perspective wrong

me cook meal to show me love her –
diplodocus with fried beans –
she say food anachronistic
but me not know what this means

stone age mighty hard for lovers
yet rub two flints look what you get
small sparks lead to big inferno
but she say love invent not yet

Note: According to Brian Bilston this was written around 1.5 million years ago by one of our earliest ancestors, *homo unrequitus*. Translated by Brian Bilston, it is considered to be the world's oldest surviving love poem.

Brian Bilston / Paul Millicheap (b.1970)

13 OCTOBER

To Celia

Drink to me only with thine eyes,
    And I will pledge with mine;
Or leave a kiss but in the cup,
    And I'll not look for wine.
The thirst that from the soul doth rise
    Doth ask a drink divine;
But might I of Jove's nectar sup,
    I would not change for thine.

I sent thee late a rosy wreath,
    Not so much honouring thee
As giving it a hope, that there
    It could not wither'd be.
But thou thereon didst only breathe,
    And sent'st it back to me;
Since when it grows, and smells, I swear,
    Not of itself, but thee!

Ben Jonson (1572–1637)

14 OCTOBER

The Sentimentalist

There lies a photograph of you
    Deep in a box of broken things.
This was the face I loved and knew
    Five years ago, when life had wings;

Five years ago, when through a town
    Of bright and soft and shadowy bowers
We walked and talked and trailed our gown
    Regardless of the cinctured hours.

The precepts that we held I kept;
    Proudly my ways with you I went:
We lived our dreams while others slept,
    And did not shrink from sentiment.

Now I go East and you stay West
    And when between us Europe lies
I shall forget what I loved best,
    Away from lips and hands and eyes.

But we were Gods then: we were they
    Who laughed at fools, believed in friends,
And drank to all that golden day
    Before us, which this poem ends.

James Elroy Flecker (1884–1915)

15 OCTOBER

Ae Fond Kiss

Ae fond kiss, and then we sever!
Ae fareweel, alas, for ever!
Deep in heart-wrung tears I'll pledge thee,
Warring sighs and groans I'll wage thee.
Who shall say that fortune grieves him,
While the star of hope she leaves him?
Me, nae cheerfu' twinkle lights me;
Dark despair around benights me.

I'll ne'er blame my partial fancy,
Naething could resist my Nancy;
But to see her was to love her;
Love but her, and love for ever.
Had we never lov'd sae kindly,
Had we never lov'd sae blindly,
Never met – or never parted –
We had ne'er been broken-hearted.

Fare thee weel, thou first and fairest!
Fare thee weel, thou best and dearest!
Thine be ilka joy and treasure,
Peace. enjoyment, love, and pleasure.
Ae fond kiss, and then we sever;
Ae fareweel, alas, for ever!
Deep in heart-wrung tears I'll pledge thee,
Warring sighs and groans I'll wage thee.

Robert Burns (1759–1796)

16 OCTOBER

A Sigh

Gentlest Air thou breath of Lovers
   Vapour from a secret fire
Which by thee itts self discovers
   E're yett daring to aspire.

Softest Noat of whisper'd anguish
   Harmony's refindest part
Striking whilst thou seem'st to languish
   Full upon the list'ners heart.

Safest Messenger of Passion
   Stealing through a crou'd of spys
Which constrain the outward fassion
   Close the Lips and guard the Eyes.

Shapelesse Sigh we ne're can show thee
   Form'd but to assault the Ear
Yett e're to their cost they know thee
   Ev'ry Nymph may read thee here.

Anne Finch (1661–1720)

17 OCTOBER

Of Love. A Sonet

How Love came in, I do not know,
Whether by th' eye, or eare, or no:
Or whether with the soule it came
(At first) infused with the same:
Whether in part 'tis here or there,
Or, like the soule, whole every where:
This troubles me: but I as well
As any other this can tell;
That when from hence she does depart
The out-let then is from the heart.

Robert Herrick (1591–1674)

18 OCTOBER

Song

Love is a startled bird that sings
    Through a slanting fall of rain.
Love is a bell in the heart that rings
    And echoes through the brain
Long after chiming. Love is a wind
    Spicy and keen and cool.
Love is a silver fish, bright finned,
    That swims in a secret pool.
Love is an apple too far to reach
    High on the orchard tree.
Love is a shell on a lonely beach
    Washed by the tide to me.

Rachel Field (1894–1942)

19 OCTOBER

Why So Pale and Wan, Fond Lover?

Why so pale and wan fond lover?
   Prithee why so pale?
Will, when looking well can't move her,
   Looking ill prevail?
   Prithee why so pale?

Why so dull and mute young sinner?
   Prithee why so mute?
Will, when speaking well can't win her,
   Saying nothing do't?
   Prithee why so mute?

Quit, quit for shame, this will not move,
   This cannot take her;
If of herself she will not love,
   Nothing can make her;
   – The devil take her!

Sir John Suckling (1609–1642)

20 OCTOBER

Echo

Come to me in the silence of the night;
　Come in the speaking silence of a dream;
Come with soft rounded cheeks and eyes as bright
　As sunlight on a stream;
　　Come back in tears,
O memory, hope, love of finished years.

Oh dream how sweet, too sweet, too bitter sweet,
　Whose wakening should have been in Paradise,
Where souls brimfull of love abide and meet;
　Where thirsting longing eyes
　　Watch the slow door
That opening, letting in, lets out no more.

Yet come to me in dreams, that I may live
　My very life again tho' cold in death:
Come back to me in dreams, that I may give
　Pulse for pulse, breath for breath:
　　Speak low, lean low,
As long ago, my love, how long ago.

Christina Rossetti (1830–1894)

21 OCTOBER

Loss

The day he moved out was terrible –
That evening she went through hell.
His absence wasn't a problem
But the corkscrew had gone as well.

Wendy Cope (b.1945)

22 OCTOBER

And You, Helen

And you, Helen, what should I give you?
So many things I would give you
Had I an infinite great store
Offered me and I stood before
To choose. I would give you youth,
All kinds of loveliness and truth,
A clear eye as good as mine,
Lands, waters, flowers, wine,
As many children as your heart
Might wish for, a far better art
Than mine can be, all you have lost
Upon the travelling waters tossed,
Or given to me. If I could choose
Freely in that great treasure-house
Anything from any shelf,
I would give you back yourself,
And power to discriminate
What you want and want it not too late,
Many fair days free from care
And heart to enjoy both foul and fair,
And myself, too, if I could find
Where it lay hidden and it proved kind.

Edward Thomas (1878–1917)

23 OCTOBER

Colin's Passion of Love

O gentle Love, ungentle for thy deed,
   Thou makest my heart
   A bloody mark
With piercing shot to bleed.

Shoot soft, sweet Love, for fear thou shoot amiss,
   For fear too keen
   Thy arrows been,
And hit the heart where my beloved is.

Too fair that fortune were, nor never I
   Shall be so blessed,
   Among the rest,
That Love shall seize on her by sympathy.

Then since with Love my prayers bear no boot,
   This doth remain
   To cease my pain,
I take the wound, and die at Venus' foot.

George Peele (1556–1596)

24 OCTOBER

La Belle Dame sans Merci: A Ballad

O what can ail thee, knight-at-arms,
    Alone and palely loitering?
The sedge has withered from the lake,
    And no birds sing.

O what can ail thee, knight-at-arms,
    So haggard and so woe-begone?
The squirrel's granary is full,
    And the harvest's done.

I see a lily on thy brow,
    With anguish moist and fever-dew,
And on thy cheeks a fading rose
    Fast withereth too.

I met a lady in the meads,
    Full beautiful – a faery's child,
Her hair was long, her foot was light,
    And her eyes were wild.

I made a garland for her head,
    And bracelets too, and fragrant zone;
She looked at me as she did love,
    And made sweet moan

I set her on my pacing steed,
    And nothing else saw all day long,
For sidelong would she bend, and sing
    A faery's song.

She found me roots of relish sweet,
    And honey wild, and manna-dew,
And sure in language strange she said –
    'I love thee true'.

She took me to her elfin grot,
    And there she wept and sighed full sore,
And there I shut her wild wild eyes
    With kisses four.

And there she lullèd me asleep,
    And there I dreamed – Ah! woe betide! –
The latest dream I ever dreamt
    On the cold hill side.

I saw pale kings and princes too,
    Pale warriors, death-pale were they all;
They cried – 'La Belle Dame sans Merci
    Thee hath in thrall!'

I saw their starved lips in the gloam,
    With horrid warning gapèd wide,
And I awoke and found me here,
    On the cold hill's side.

And this is why I sojourn here,
    Alone and palely loitering,
Though the sedge is withered from the lake,
    And no birds sing.

John Keats (1795–1821)

25 OCTOBER

Air IV

FROM *THE BEGGAR'S OPERA*, ACT I, SCENE IV

If love the virgin's heart invade,
How, like a moth, the simple maid
    Still plays about the flame!
If soon she be not made a wife,
Her honour's singed, and then for life
    She's – what I dare not name.

John Gay (1685–1732)

26 OCTOBER

Incompatibilities

If you loved me I could trust you to your fancy's furthest
    bound
While the sun shone and the wind blew, and the world
    went round,
To the utmost of the meshes of the devil's strongest net . . .
If you loved me, if you loved me – but you do not love me yet!

I love you – and I cannot trust you further than the door!
But winds and worlds and seasons change, and you will love
    me more
And more – until I trust you, dear, as women do trust men –
I shall trust you, I shall trust you, but I shall not love you then!

E. Nesbit (1858–1924)

27 OCTOBER

Alas! madam, for stelyng of a kisse

Alas! madame, for stelyng of a kisse
   Have I so much your mynd there offended?
Have I then done so grevously amysse
   That by no means it may be amended?
Then revenge you, and the next way is this:
   An other kysse shall have my lyffe endid,
For to my mowth the first my hert did suck,
The next shall clene out of my brest it pluck.

Sir Thomas Wyatt (1503–1542)

28 OCTOBER

To My Wife – with a Copy of my Poems

I can write no stately proem
   As a prelude to my lay;
From a poet to a poem
   I would dare to say.

For if of these fallen petals
   One to you seem fair,
Love will waft it till it settles
   On your hair.

And when wind and winter harden
   All the loveless land,
It will whisper of the garden,
   You will understand.

Oscar Wilde (1854–1900)

29 OCTOBER

Renouncement

I must not think of thee; and, tired yet strong,
   I shun the thought that lurks in all delight–
   The thought of thee – and in the blue Heaven's height,
And in the sweetest passage of a song.
Oh, just beyond the fairest thoughts that throng
   This breast, the thought of thee waits hidden yet bright;
   But it must never, never come in sight;
I must stop short of thee the whole day long.

But when sleep comes to close each difficult day,
   When night gives pause to the long watch I keep,
   And all my bonds I needs must loose apart,
Must doff my will as raiment laid away,–
   With the first dream that comes with the first sleep
   I run, I run, I am gathered to thy heart.

Alice Meynell (1847–1922)

30 OCTOBER

To His Coy Love: A Canzonet

I pray thee leave, love me no more,
   Call home the heart you gave me:
I but in vain that saint adore,
   That can, but will not, save me:
These poor half kisses kill me quite;
   Was ever man thus servèd?
Amidst an ocean of delight
   For pleasure to be starvèd.

Show me no more those snowy breasts
   With azure riverets branchèd,
Where whilst mine eye with plenty feasts,
   Yet is my thirst not stanchèd.
O Tantalus, thy pains ne'er tell,
   By me thou art prevented:
'Tis nothing to be plagued in hell,
   But thus in heaven tormented.

Clip me no more in those dear arms,
   Nor thy life's comfort call me;
O, these are but too pow'rful charms,
   And do but more enthral me.
But see how patient I am grown,
   In all this coil about thee;
Come, nice thing, let my heart alone,
   I cannot live without thee.

Michael Drayton (1563–1631)

31 OCTOBER

Except for the Body

Except for the body
of someone you love,
including all its expressions
in privacy and in public,

trees, I think,
are the most beautiful
forms on the earth.

Though, admittedly,
if this were a contest,
the trees would come in
an extremely distant second.

Mary Oliver (1935–2019)

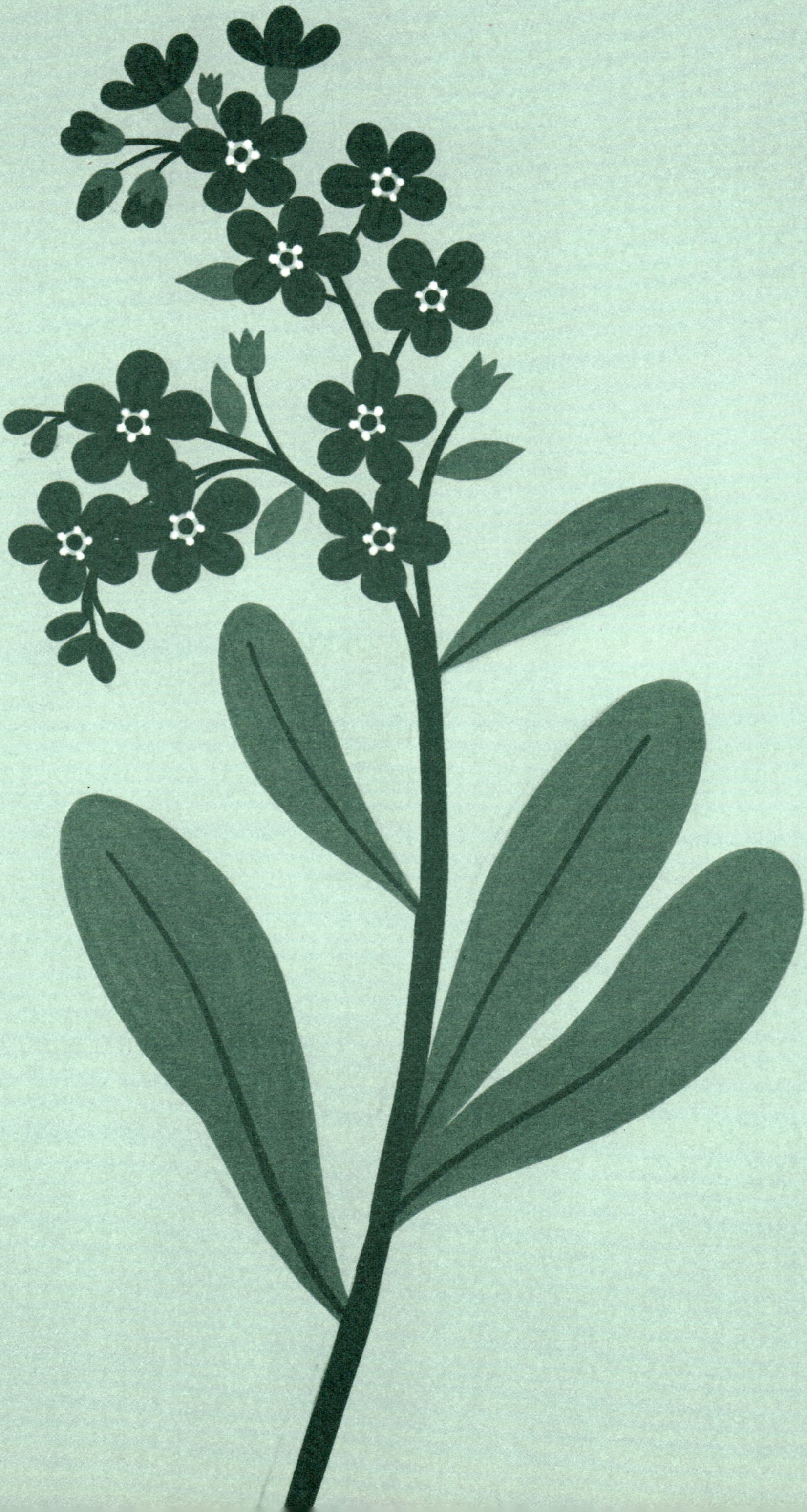

NOVEMBER

Life of My Life

1 NOVEMBER

Sonnet 73

That time of year thou mayst in me behold
When yellow leaves, or none, or few, do hang
Upon those boughs which shake against the cold,
Bare ruined choirs, where late the sweet birds sang.
In me thou seest the twilight of such day
As after sunset fadeth in the west,
Which by and by black night doth take away,
Death's second self, that seals up all in rest.
In me thou seest the glowing of such fire
That on the ashes of his youth doth lie,
As the death-bed whereon it must expire,
Consumed with that which it was nourished by.
   This thou perceiv'st, which makes thy love more strong,
   To love that well which thou must leave ere long.

William Shakespeare (1564–1616)

2 NOVEMBER

Play-Acting

Morning drops down
As the curtain rises;
Somewhere, off-stage,
The sun is shining.
And in the wings, out of sight,
Someone gives stage directions,
Pulls the strings.
You put on your mask
And say you love me:
Lines you know by heart.
Still, I must congratulate you on
How well you play your part.
You always did like to be centre-stage;
The lead character in the play;
The darling of the theatre;
The limelight was ever
Your element.
And between the *trompe l'oeil*
Of the scenery
And your plausible sincerity,
It is hard to separate
Make-believe from reality;
Romance, from performance;
The truth, from the lie.
But when night falls,
With a roll of drums,
A paper moon hangs,
In a paper sky.

Jana Synková (b.1968)

3 NOVEMBER

Song

When I am dead, my dearest,
   Sing no sad songs for me;
Plant thou no roses at my head,
   Nor shady cypress tree:
Be the green grass above me
   With showers and dewdrops wet;
And if thou wilt, remember,
   And if thou wilt, forget.

I shall not see the shadows,
   I shall not feel the rain;
I shall not hear the nightingale
   Sing on, as if in pain:
And dreaming through the twilight
   That doth not rise nor set,
Haply I may remember,
   And haply may forget.

Christina Rossetti (1830–1894)

4 NOVEMBER

Paradise
FROM EDWARD FITZGERALD'S TRANSLATION
OF *THE RUBÁIYÁT OF OMAR KHAYYÁM*, 1859

Here with a Loaf of Bread beneath the Bough,
A Flask of Wine, a Book of Verse – and Thou
   Beside me singing in the Wilderness –
And Wilderness is Paradise enow.

'How sweet is mortal Sovranty! – think some:
Others – 'How blest the Paradise to come!'
   Ah, take the Cash in hand and waive the Rest;
Oh, the brave Music of a *distant* Drum!

Look to the Rose that blows about us – 'Lo,
Laughing,' she says, 'into the World I blow:
   At once the silken Tassel of my Purse
Tear, and its Treasure on the Garden throw.'

The Worldly Hope men set their Hearts upon
Turns Ashes – or it prospers; and anon,
   Like Snow upon the Desert's dusty Face
Lighting a little Hour or two – is gone.

Omar ibn Ibrahim al-Khayyám (1048–1131)
translated by **Edward Fitzgerald (1809–1883)**

5 NOVEMBER

Womankind

Dear things! we would not have you learn too much –
   Your Ignorance is so charming! We've a notion
That greater knowledge might not lend you such
   Sure aid to blind obedience and devotion.

Gerald Massey (1820–1907)

6 NOVEMBER

Erasure

Falling out of love
is a rusty chain going quickly through a winch.
It hurts more than you will remember.
It costs a pint of blood turned grey
and burning out a few high paths
among the glittering synapses of the brain,
a few stars fading out at once in the galaxy,
a configuration gone
imagination called a lion or a dragon or a sunburst
that would photograph more like a blurry mouse.
When falling out of love is correcting vision
light grates on the eyes
light files the optic nerve hot and raw.
To find you have loved a coward and a fool
is to give up the lion, the dragon, the sunburst
and take away your hands covered with small festering bites
and let the mouse go in a grey blur
into the baseboard.

Marge Piercy (b.1936)

7 NOVEMBER

Last

Friend, whose smile has come to be
Very precious unto me,
   Though I know I drank not first
   Of your love's bright fountain-burst,
Yet I grieve not for the past,
So you only love me last!

Other souls may find their joy
In the blind love of a boy:
   Give me that which years have tried,
   Disciplined and purified, –
Such as, braving sun and blast,
You will bring to me at last!

There are brows more fair than mine,
Eyes of more bewitching shine,
   Other hearts more fit, in truth,
   For the passion of your youth;
But, their transient empire past,
You will surely love me last!

Wing away your summer-time,
Find a love in every clime,
   Roam in liberty and light, –
   I shall never stay your flight;
For I know, when all is past,
You will come to me at last!

Change and flutter as you will,
I shall smile securely still;
   Patiently I trust and wait
   Though you tarry long and late;
Prize your spring till it be past,
Only, only love me last!

Elizabeth Akers Allen (1832–1911)

8 NOVEMBER

A Modest Love

The lowest trees have tops, the ant her gall,
   The fly her spleen, the little sparks their heat;
The slender hairs cast shadows, though but small,
   And bees have stings, although they be not great;
Seas have their source, and so have shallow springs;
And love is love, in beggars as in kings.

Where rivers smoothest run, deep are the fords;
   The dial stirs, yet none perceives it move;
The firmest faith is in the fewest words;
   The turtles cannot sing, and yet they love:
True hearts have eyes and ears, no tongues to speak;
They hear and see, and sigh, and then they break.

Sir Edward Dyer (1543–1607)

9 NOVEMBER

Brown Penny

I whispered, 'I am too young,'
And then, 'I am old enough';
Wherefore I threw a penny
To find out if I might love.
'Go and love, go and love, young man,
If the lady be young and fair.'
Ah, penny, brown penny, brown penny,
I am looped in the loops of her hair.
And the penny sang up in my face,
'There is nobody wise enough
To find out all that is in it,
For he would be thinking of love
That is looped in the loops of her hair,
Till the loops of time had run.'
Ah, penny, brown penny, brown penny,
One cannot begin it too soon.

W. B. Yeats (1865–1939)

10 NOVEMBER

I cry your mercy, pity – love – aye, love!

I cry your mercy, pity – love – aye, love!
   Merciful love that tantalizes not,
One-thoughted, never-wandering, guileless love,
   Unmasked, and being seen – without a blot!
O! let me have thee whole, – all, all, be mine!
   That shape, that fairness, that sweet minor zest
Of love, your kiss – those hands, those eyes divine,
   That warm, white, lucent, million-pleasured breast –
Yourself – your soul – in pity give me all,
   Withhold no atom's atom or I die;
Or living on perhaps, your wretched thrall,
   Forget, in the mist of idle misery,
Life's purposes – the palate of my mind
Losing its gust, and my ambition blind!

John Keats (1795–1821)

11 NOVEMBER

Appraisal

Never think she loves him wholly,
Never believe her love is blind,
All his faults are locked securely
In a closet of her mind;
All his indecisions folded
Like old flags that time has faded,
Limp and streaked with rain,
And his cautiousness like garments
Frayed and thin, with many a stain –
Let them be, oh, let them be,
There is treasure to outweigh them,
His proud will that sharply stirred,
Climbs as surely as the tide,
Senses strained too taut to sleep,
Gentleness to beast and bird,
Humor flickering hushed and wide
As the moon on moving water,
And a tenderness too deep
To be gathered in a word.

Sara Teasdale (1884–1933)

12 NOVEMBER

Song

Love for such a cherry lip
   Would be glad to pawn his arrows;
Venus here to take a sip
   Would sell her doves and teams of sparrows.
      But they shall not so;
         Hey nonny, nonny no!
      None but I this lip must owe,
         Hey nonny, nonny no!

Did Jove see this wanton eye,
   Ganymede must wait no longer;
Phoebe here one night did lie,
   Would change her face and look much younger.
      But they shall not so;
         Hey nonny, nonny no!
      None but I this lip must owe;
         Hey nonny, nonny no!

Thomas Middleton (1580–1627)

13 NOVEMBER

On the Beach at Fontana

Wind whines and whines the shingle,
The crazy pierstakes groan;
A senile sea numbers each single
Slimesilvered stone.

From whining wind and colder
Grey sea I wrap him warm
And touch his trembling fineboned shoulder
And boyish arm.

Around us fear, descending
Darkness of fear above
And in my heart how deep unending
Ache of love!

Trieste, 1914

James Joyce (1882–1941)

14 NOVEMBER

I loved you first: but afterwards your love

'POCA FAVILLA GRAN FIAMMA SECONDA.' – DANTE
'OGNI ALTRA COSA, OGNI PENSIER VA FORE,
E SOL IVI CON VOI RIMANSI AMORE.' – PETRARCA
FROM *MONNA INNOMINATA: A SONNET OF SONNETS*

I loved you first: but afterwards your love
   Outsoaring mine, sang such a loftier song
As drowned the friendly cooings of my dove.
   Which owes the other most? my love was long,
   And yours one moment seemed to wax more strong;
I loved and guessed at you, you construed me
And loved me for what might or might not be –
   Nay, weights and measures do us both a wrong.
For verily love knows not 'mine' or 'thine;'
   With separate 'I' and 'thou' free love has done,
     For one is both and both are one in love:
Rich love knows nought of 'thine that is not mine;'
     Both have the strength and both the length thereof,
Both of us, of the love which makes us one.

Christina Rossetti (1830–1894)

15 NOVEMBER

To –

Music, when soft voices die,
Vibrates in the memory –
Odours, when sweet violets sicken,
Live within the sense they quicken.

Rose leaves, when the rose is dead,
Are heaped for the belovèd's bed;
And so thy thoughts, when thou art gone,
Love itself shall slumber on.

Percy Bysshe Shelley (1792–1822)

16 NOVEMBER

The Chilterns

Your hands, my dear, adorable,
   Your lips of tenderness
– Oh, I've loved you faithfully and well,
   Three years, or a bit less.
   It wasn't a success.

Thank God, that's done! and I'll take the road,
   Quit of my youth and you,
The Roman road to Wendover
   By Tring and Lilley Hoo,
   As a free man may do.

For youth goes over, the joys that fly,
   The tears that follow fast;
And the dirtiest things we do must lie
   Forgotten at the last;
   Even Love goes past.

What's left behind I shall not find,
   The splendour and the pain;
The splash of sun, the shouting wind,
   And the brave sting of rain,
   I may not meet again.

But the years, that take the best away,
   Give something in the end;
And a better friend than love have they,
   For none to mar or mend,
   That have themselves to friend.

I shall desire and I shall find
   The best of my desires;
The autumn road, the mellow wind
   That soothes the darkening shires.
   And laughter, and inn-fires.

White mist about the black hedgerows,
   The slumbering Midland plain,
The silence where the clover grows,
   And the dead leaves in the lane,
   Certainly, these remain.

And I shall find some girl perhaps,
   And a better one than you,
With eyes as wise, but kindlier,
   And lips as soft, but true.
   And I daresay she will do.

Rupert Brooke (1887–1915)

17 NOVEMBER

Sweet mother

Sweet mother, I can't take shuttle in hand.
There is a boy, and lust
Has crushed my spirit – just
As gentle Aphrodite planned.

Since I have cast my lot, please, golden-crowned
Aphrodite, let me win this round!

Sappho (c.630 BCE – c.570 CE)
translated by **Aaron Poochigian (b.1973)**

18 november

may I feel said he

may i feel said he
(i'll squeal said she
just once said he)
it's fun said she

(may i touch said he
how much said she
a lot said he)
why not said she

(let's go said he
not too far said she
what's too far said he
where you are said she)

may i stay said he
(which way said she
like this said he
if you kiss said she

may i move said he
is it love said she)
if you're willing said he
(but you're killing said she

but it's life said he
but your wife said she
now said he)
ow said she

(tiptop said he
don't stop said she
oh no said he)
go slow said she

(cccome?said he
ummm said she)
you're divine!said he
(you are Mine said she)

e.e. cummings (1894–1962)

19 NOVEMBER

Brother and Sister

VERSE I

I cannot choose but think upon the time
When our two lives grew like two buds that kiss
At lightest thrill from the bee's swinging chime.
Because the one so near the other is.

He was the elder and a little man
Of forty inches, bound to show no dread,
And I the girl that puppy-like now ran.
Now lagged behind my brother's larger tread.

I held him wise, and when he talked to me
Of snakes and birds, and which God loved the best,
I thought his knowledge marked the boundary
Where men grew blind, though angels knew the rest.

If he said 'Hush!' I tried to hold my breath;
Wherever he said 'Come!' I stepped in faith.

George Eliot (1819–1880)

20 NOVEMBER

Love in all Colours

If I could make a love
quilt
I'd start with peppermint
then add chocolate
in the stripes

My favorite fruit
is Blackberry
but we need a lot of sugar
on them

I guess the quilt
is not edible
but if I could eat
it
I'd have fried okra
and a couple of home fried
chicken wings
with whole garlic cloves
and ginger root
in butter

This is probably not
what Love they had
in mind
but it is what I Love

So I can either eat
or snuggle
with the love
of my Life

Nikki Giovanni (b.1943)

21 NOVEMBER

Claude to Eustace X

FROM *AMOURS DU VOYAGE*, CANTO II

I am in love, meantime, you think; no doubt you would think so.
I am in love, you say; with those letters, of course, you would say so.
I am in love, you declare. I think not so; yet I grant you
It is a pleasure indeed to converse with this girl. Oh, rare gift,
Rare felicity, this! she can talk in a rational way, can
Speak upon subjects that really are matters of mind and of thinking,
Yet in perfection retain her simplicity; never, one moment,
Never, however you urge it, however you tempt her, consents to
Step from ideas and fancies and loving sensations to those vain
Conscious understandings that vex the minds of man-kind.
No, though she talk, it is music; her fingers desert not the keys; 'tis
Song, though you hear in the song the articulate vocables sounded,
Syllabled singly and sweetly the words of melodious meaning.
    I am in love, you say; I do not think so, exactly.

Arthur Hugh Clough (1819–1861)

22 NOVEMBER

Autumn

When autumn winds are on the hill
   And darkly rides the wasting moon,
I creep within your arms, and still
   Am safe in the golden heart of June.

Mary Webb (1881–1927)

23 NOVEMBER

The Fair Singer

i
To make a final conquest of all me,
Love did compose so sweet an Enemy,
In whom both Beauties to my death agree,
Joining themselves in fatal Harmony;
That while she with her Eyes my Heart does bind,
She with her Voice might captivate my Mind.

ii
I could have fled from One but singly fair,
My dis-entangled Soul itself might save,
Breaking the curled trammels of her hair.
But how should I avoid to be her Slave,
Whose subtile Art invisibly can wreath
My Fetters of the very Air I breathe?

iii
It had been easie fighting in some plain,
Where Victory might hang in equal choice,
But all resistance against her is vain,
Who has th'advantage both of Eyes and Voice,
And all my Forces needs must be undone,
She having gained both the Wind and Sun.

Andrew Marvell (1621–1678)

24 NOVEMBER

I think I should have loved you presently

I think I should have loved you presently,
And given in earnest words I flung in jest;
And lifted honest eyes for you to see,
And caught your hand against my cheek and breast;
And all my pretty follies flung aside
That won you to me, and beneath your gaze,
Naked of reticence and shorn of pride,
Spread like a chart my little wicked ways.
I, that had been to you, had you remained,
But one more waking from a recurrent dream,
Cherish no less the certain stakes I gained,
And walk your memory's halls, austere, supreme,
A ghost in marble of a girl you knew
Who would have loved you in a day or two.

Edna St Vincent Millay (1892–1950)

25 NOVEMBER

A Song of a Young Lady to her Ancient Lover

Ancient person, for whom I
All the flattering youth defy,
Long be it ere thou grow old,
Aching, shaking, crazy, cold;
But still continue as thou art,
   Ancient Person of my heart.

On thy withered lips and dry,
Which like barren furrows lie,
Brooding kisses I will pour
Shall thy youthful heat restore
Such kind showers in autumn fall,
And a second spring recall:
Nor from thee will ever part,
   Ancient Person of my heart.

Thy nobler part, which but to name
In our sex would be counted shame,
By age's frozen grasp possessed,
From [his] ice shall be released,
And, soothed by my reviving hand,
In former warmth and vigour stand.
All a lover's wish can reach
For thy joy my love shall teach,
And for they pleasure shall improve
All that art can add to love.
Yet still I love thee without art,
   Ancient Person of my heart.

John Wilmot, Lord Rochester (1647–1680)

26 NOVEMBER

Words, Wide Night

Somewhere on the other side of this wide night
and the distance between us, I am thinking of you.
The room is turning slowly away from the moon.

This is pleasurable. Or shall I cross that out and say
it is sad? In one of the tenses I singing
an impossible song of desire that you cannot hear.

La lala la. See? I close my eyes and imagine
the dark hills I would have to cross
to reach you. For I am in love with you and this

is what it is like or what it is like in words.

Carol Ann Duffy (b.1955)

27 NOVEMBER

Sonnet 11

FROM *CYNTHIA*

Sighing, and sadly sitting by my Love,
   He ask't the cause of my hearts sorrowing,
   Conjuring me by heavens eternall King
To tell the cause which me so much did move.
Compell'd (quoth I), to thee will I confesse,
   Love is the cause, and onely love it is
   That doth deprive me of my heavenly blisse.
Love is the paine that doth my heart oppresse.
And what is she (quoth he) whom thou do'st love?
   Looke in this glasse (quoth I), there shalt thou see
   The perfect form of my fælicitie.
When, thinking that it would strange Magique prove,
   He open'd it: and taking off the cover,
   He straight perceav'd himselfe to be my Lover.

Richard Barnfield (c.1574–1620)

28 NOVEMBER

When I Heard at the Close of the Day

When I heard at the close of the day how my name had been receiv'd with plaudits in the capitol, still it was not a happy night for me that follow'd,
And else when I carous'd, or when my plans were accomplish'd, still I was not happy,
But the day when I rose at dawn from the bed of perfect health, refresh'd, singing, inhaling the ripe breath of autumn,
When I saw the full moon in the west grow pale and disappear in the morning light,
When I wander'd alone over the beach, and undressing bathed, laughing with the cool waters, and saw the sun rise,
And when I thought how my dear friend my lover was on his way coming, O then I was happy,
O then each breath tasted sweeter, and all that day my food nourish'd me more, and the beautiful day pass'd well,
And the next came with equal joy, and with the next at evening came my friend,
And that night, while all was still I heard the waters roll slowly continually up the shores,
I heard the hissing rustle of the liquid and sands as directed to me whispering to congratulate me,
For the one I love most lay sleeping by me under the same cover in the cool night,
In the stillness in the autumn moonbeams his face was inclined toward me,
And his arm lay lightly around my breast—and that night I was happy.

Walt Whitman (1819–1892)

29 NOVEMBER

A Song

Ask me no more where Jove bestows,
When June is past, the fading rose;
For in your beauty's orient deep
These flowers, as in their causes, sleep.

Ask me no more whither do stray
The golden atoms of the day;
For in pure love heaven did prepare
Those powders to enrich your hair.

Ask me no more whither doth haste
The nightingale, when May is past;
For in your sweet dividing throat
She winters, and keeps warm her note.

Ask me no more where those stars light,
That downwards fall in dead of night;
For in your eyes they sit, and there
Fixèd become, as in their sphere.

Ask me no more if east or west
The phoenix builds her spicy nest;
For unto you at last she flies,
And in your fragrant bosom dies.

Thomas Carew (1595–1640)

30 NOVEMBER

XXVII

FROM *IN MEMORIAM A. H. H.*

I envy not in any moods
   The captive void of noble rage,
   The linnet born within the cage,
That never knew the summer woods:

I envy not the beast that takes
   His license in the field of time,
   Unfettered by the sense of crime,
To whom a conscience never wakes;

Nor, what may count itself as blest,
   The heart that never plighted troth
   But stagnates in the weeds of sloth;
Nor any want-begotten rest.

I hold it true, what e'er befall;
   I feel it when I sorrow most;
   'Tis better to have loved and lost
Than never to have loved at all.

Alfred, Lord Tennyson (1809–1892)

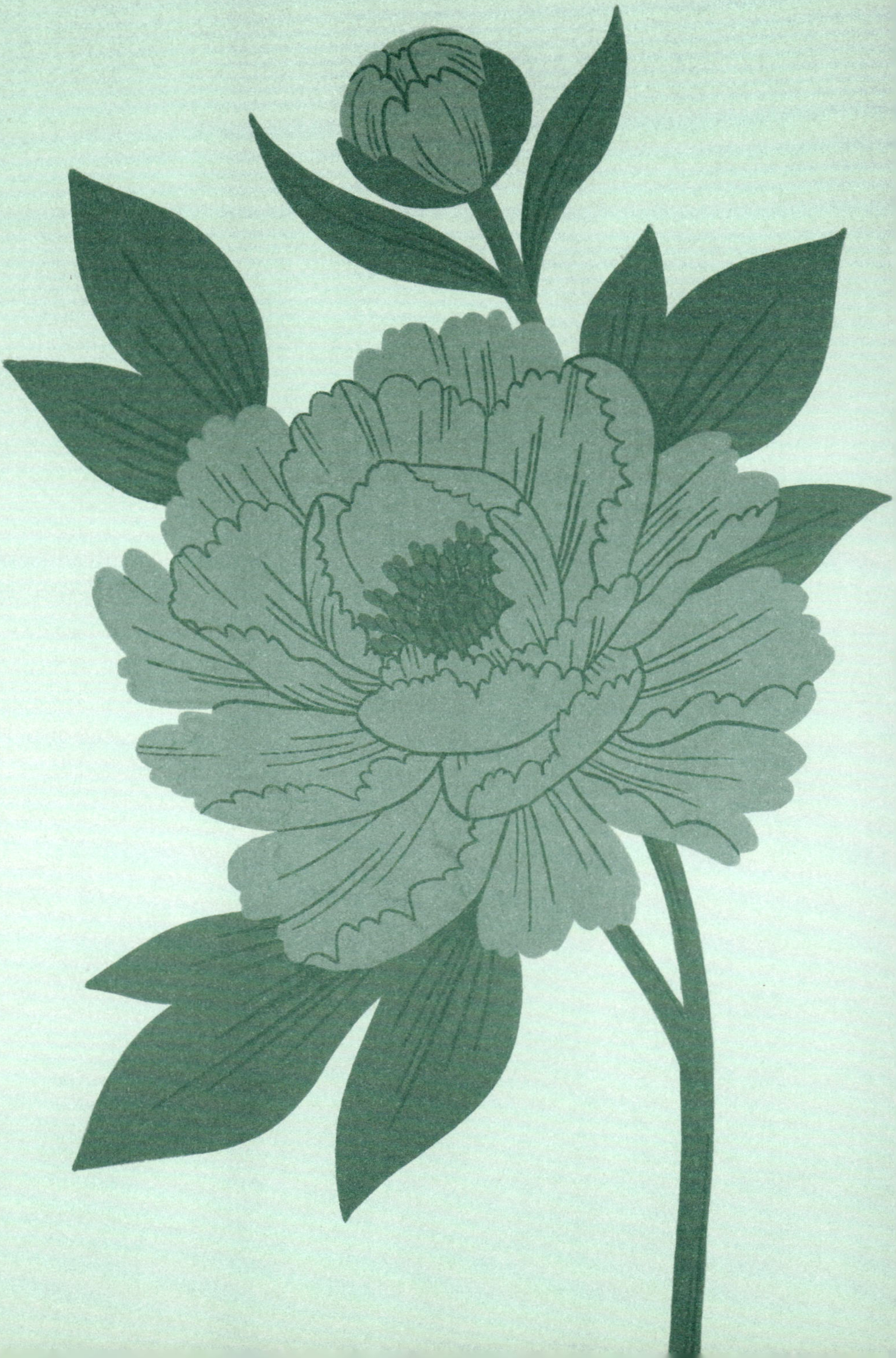

DECEMBER

Thy Heart is Mine

1 DECEMBER

Winter Song

Ask me no more, my Truth to prove,
What I wou'd suffer for my Love:
With thee I wou'd in Exile go,
To Regions of eternal Snow,
O'er Floods by solid ice confin'd,
Through Forest bare with Northern Wind:
While all around my Eyes I cast,
Where all is wild and all is waste.
If there the tim'rous Stag you chase,
Or rouse to fight a fiercer Race,
Undaunted I thy Arms wou'd bear,
And give thy Hand the Hunter's Spear.
When the low Sun withdraws his Light,
And menaces an half Year's Night,
The conscious Moon and Stars above
Shall guide me with my wand'ring Love.
Beneath the Mountain's hollow Brow,
Or in its rocky Cells below,
Thy rural Feast I wou'd provide.
Nor envy Palaces their Pride.
The softest Moss should dress thy Bed,
With Savage Spoils about thee spread:
While faithful Love the Watch should keep,
To banish Danger from thy Sleep.

Elizabeth Tollet (1694–1754)

2 DECEMBER

It chanced that Cupid
FROM THE FRENCH

It chanced that Cupid on a season.
   By Fancy urged resolved to wed,
But could not settle whether Reason
   Or Folly should partake his bed.

What does he then? – Upon my life,
   'Twas bad example for a deity –
He takes me Reason for a wife,
   And Folly for his hours of gaiety.

Though thus he dealt in petty treason.
   He loved them both in equal measure;
Fidelity was born of Reason,
   And Folly brought to bed of Pleasure.

Sir Walter Scott (1771–1832)

3 DECEMBER

What lips my lips have kissed

What lips my lips have kissed, and where, and why,
I have forgotten, and what arms have lain
Under my head till morning; but the rain
Is full of ghosts tonight, that tap and sigh
Upon the glass and listen for reply,
And in my heart there stirs a quiet pain
For unremembered lads that not again
Will turn to me at midnight with a cry.
Thus in the winter stands the lonely tree,
Nor knows what birds have vanished one by one,
Yet knows its boughs more silent than before:
I cannot say what loves have come and gone,
I only know that summer sang in me
A little while, that in me sings no more.

Edna St Vincent Millay (1892–1950)

4 DECEMBER

An Appeal to Cats in the Business of Love

Ye cats that at midnight spit love at each other,
Who best feel the pangs of a passionate lover,
I appeal to your scratches and your tattered fur,
If the business of Love be no more than to purr.
Old Lady Grimalkin with her gooseberry eyes,
Knew something when a kitten, for why she was wise;
You find by experience, the love-fit's soon o'er,
Puss! Puss! lasts not long, but turns to *Cat-whore!*
   Men ride many miles,
   Cats tread many tiles,
Both hazard their necks in the fray;
   Only Cats, when they fall
   From a house or a wall,
Keep their feet, mount their tails, and away!

Thomas Flatman (1637–1688)

5 DECEMBER

The admonition by the Auctor

TO ALL YOUNG GENTILWOMEN:
AND TO AL OTHER MAIDS BEING IN LOVE

Ye Virgins that from Cupids tentes
   do beare away the soyle
Whose hartes as yet with raginge love
   most paynfully do boyle.

To you I speak: for you be they
   that good advice do lacke:
Oh, if I could good counsell geve
   my tongue should not be slacke?

But such as I can geve, I wyll
   here in few wordes expresse:
Which, if you do observe, it will
   some of your care redresse.

Beware of fayre and painted talke,
   beware of flattering tongues:
The Mermaides do pretend no good
   for all their pleasant songs.

Some use the tears of crocodiles,
   contrary to their hart:
And yf they cannot alwayes weepe,
   they wet their Cheeks by Art.

Ovid, within his Arte of Love,
   doth teach them this same knacke
To wet their hand and touch their eies,
   so oft as teares they lacke.

Why have ye such deceit in store?
   have you such crafty wile?
Lesse craft than this, God knows, wold soone
   us simple soules begile.

And will ye not leave off? but still
   delude us in this wise?
Sith it is so, we trust we shall
   take hede to fained lies.

Trust not a man at the fyrst sight
   but trye him well before:
I wish al Maids within their brests
   to kepe this thing in store.

For triall shall declare his trueth
   and show what he doth think,
Whether he be a Lover true,
   or do intend to shrink.

Isabella Whitney (c.1566–1600)

6 DECEMBER

The Look

Strephon kissed me in the spring,
    Robin in the fall,
But Colin only looked at me
    And never kissed at all.

Strephon's kiss was lost in jest,
    Robin's lost in play,
But the kiss in Colin's eyes
    Haunts me night and day.

Sara Teasdale (1884–1933)

7 DECEMBER

Surrender

Oh, the nights were dark and cold,
    When my love was gone.
And life was hard to hold
    When my love was gone.
I was wise, I never gave
What they teach a girl to save,
But I wished myself his slave
    When my love was gone.

I was all alone at night
    When my love came home.
Oh, what thought of wrong or right
    When my love came home?
I flung the door back wide
And I pulled my love inside;
There was no more shame or pride
    When my love came home.

E. Nesbit (1858–1924)

8 december

At the entrance of the café

My attention was directed by something said beside me,
toward the entrance of the café.
And I saw that lovely body that appeared
as if created by Eros in his consummate experience –
fashioning its well-proportioned limbs with joy;
raising a sculpted posture;
fashioning the face with deep emotion
and bestowing, by the touch of his hands,
a feeling upon the brow, the eyes, and the lips.

Constantine Cavafy (1863–1993)
translated by **Evangelos Sachperoglou (b.1941)**

9 DECEMBER

The Life That I Have

The life that I have
Is all that I have
And the life that I have
Is yours.

The love that I have
Of the life that I have
Is yours and yours and yours.

A sleep I shall have
A rest I shall have
Yet death will be but a pause.

For the peace of my years
In the long green grass
Will be yours and yours and yours.

Leo Marks (1920–2001)

10 DECEMBER

To Cleon's Eyes

LINES 1-22

The love you dare but look I find:
The eyes speak best the lover's mind;
The God of Love reveals the news,
Whose dart has stamped the billet-doux;
No paper could such sweetness boast,
For half the spirit would be lost
Ere I could read that duller way,
What in a moment these convey.
Oh! let thy eyes with truth be fraught,
Mine shall repay each modest thought.
Thus souls employ their hours above,
Exchanging looks of deathless love;
In looking wondrous magic lies,
Oh! there is poetry in eyes:
Methinks I see a Waller shine
In every sparkling beam of thine;
Or when in nobler language dressed,
With Milton's spirit they are blessed:
Thus Adam tenderly surveyed
With guiltless looks the blushing maid,
Who met his eyes unskilled in art:
They were no prudes but spoke her heart.

Martha Sansom (1690-1736)

11 DECEMBER

An Ode

The merchant, to secure his treasure,
   Conveys it in a borrowed name:
Euphelia serves to grace my measure,
   But Cloe is my real flame.

My softest verse, my darling lyre
   Upon Euphelia's toilet lay –
When Cloe noted her desire
   That I should sing, that I should play.

My lyre I tune, my voice I raise,
   But with my numbers mix my sighs;
And whilst I sing Euphelia's praise,
   I fix my soul on Cloe's eyes.

Fair Cloe blushed; Euphelia frowned:
   I sung, and gazed; I played, and trembled:
And Venus to the Loves around
   Remarked how ill we all dissembled.

Matthew Prior (1664–1721)

12 DECEMBER

Sonnet

FROM *LA VITA NUOVA*

Love and the gentle heart are one same thing,
    Even as the wise man in his ditty saith:
    Each, of itself, would be such life in death
As rational soul bereft of reasoning.
'Tis Nature makes them when she loves: a king
    Love is, whose palace where he sojourneth
    Is called the Heart; there draws he quiet breath
At first, with brief or longer slumbering.
Then beauty seen in virtuous womankind
    Will make the eyes desire, and through the heart
    Send the desiring of the eyes again;
Where often it abides so long enshrin'd
    That Love at length out of his sleep will start.
    And women feel the same for worthy men.

Dante Alighieri (1265–1321)
translated by **Dante Gabriel Rossetti (1828–1882)**

13 DECEMBER

You

You won't believe it. Perhaps you're too prosaic
    To fall for a poetic ache,
But your smile (when you smile), your eyes, your nose,
    Are far too beautiful for prose.

Don't credit this, my dear, if you don't want to.
    A poem, too, can be a pack of lies.
But if you don't, then I'll come back and haunt you.
    You'll find me hard to exorcise.

Douglas Dunn (b.1942)

14 DECEMBER

The Unknown

She is most fair,
And when they see her pass
The poets' ladies
Look no more in the glass
But after her.

On a bleak moor
Running under the moon
She lures a poet,
Once proud or happy, soon
Far from his door.

Beside a train,
Because they saw her go,
Or failed to see her,
Travellers and watchers know
Another pain.

The simple lack
Of her is more to me
Than others' presence,
Whether life splendid be
Or utter black.

I have not seen,
I have no news of her;
I can tell only
She is not here, but there
She might have been.

She is to be kissed
Only perhaps by me;
She may be seeking
Me and no other; she
May not exist.

Edward Thomas (1878–1917)

15 DECEMBER

Love me as I love thee

Love me as I love thee. O double sweet!
But if thou hate me who love thee,
   Even thus I have the better of thee:
Thou canst not hate me so much as I do love thee.

Gerard Manley Hopkins (1844–1889)

16 DECEMBER

A Drinking Song

Wine comes in at the mouth
And love comes in at the eye;
That's all we shall know for truth
Before we grow old and die.
I lift the glass to my mouth,
I look at you, and I sigh.

W. B. Yeats (1865–1939)

17 DECEMBER

The Ballad of Sally in our Alley

Of all the girls that are so smart
    There's none like pretty Sally,
She is the darling of my heart,
    And she lives in our alley.
There is no lady in the land
    Is half so sweet as Sally,
She is the darling of my heart,
    And she lives in our alley.

Her father he makes cabbage-nets,
    And through the streets does cry 'em;
Her mother she sells laces long,
    To such as please to buy 'em:
But sure such folks could ne'er beget
    So sweet a girl as Sally!
She is the darling of my heart,
    And she lives in our alley.

When she is by I leave my work,
    (I love her so sincerely)
My master comes like any Turk,
    And bangs me most severely;
But, let him bang his bellyfull,
    I'll bear it all for Sally;
She is the darling of my heart,
    And she lives in our alley.

Of all the days that's in the week,
    I dearly love but one day,
And that's the day that comes betwixt
    A Saturday and Monday;

For then I'm dressed, all in my best,
    To walk abroad with Sally;
She is the darling of my heart,
    And she lives in our alley.

My master carries me to church,
    And often am I blamed,
Because I leave him in the lurch,
    As soon as text is named:
I leave the church in sermon time,
    And slink away to Sally;
She is the darling of my heart,
    And she lives in our alley.

When Christmas comes about again,
    O then I shall have money;
I'll hoard it up, and box and all
    I'll give it to my honey:
And, would it were ten thousand pounds;
    I'd give it all to Sally;
She is the darling of my heart,
    And she lives in our alley.

My master and the neighbours all,
    Make game of me and Sally;
And, but for her, I'd better be
    A slave and row a galley:
But when my seven long years are out,
    O then I'll marry Sally!
O, then we'll wed and then we'll bed,
    But not in our alley.

Henry Carey (1687–1743)

18 December

Sonnets to Delia

(I)

Unto the boundless ocean of thy beauty
   Runs this poor river, charged with streams of zeal,
Returning thee the tribute of my duty,
   Which here my love, my youth, my plaints reveal.
Here I unclasp the book of my charged soul,
   Where I have cast th'accounts of all my care:
Here have I summed my sighs, here I enroll
   How they were spent for thee; look what they are.
Look on the dear expenses of my youth,
   And see how just I reckon with thine eyes:
Examine well thy beauty with my truth,
   And cross my cares ere greater sum arise.
      Read it sweet maid, though it be done but slightly;
      Who can show all his love, doth love but lightly.

Samuel Daniel (1562–1619)

19 DECEMBER

To My Absent Wife

My dear, true wife,
　Life of my life,
And my heart's solace only,
　Thou knowest not
　How drear my lot
Without thee, and how lonely!

　Yet well I know.
　Come weal or woe,
Thy heart is mine forever:
　Though far apart
　From me thou art,
Our true souls naught can sever!

　What though the pall
　Of sorrow fall,
And shroud all things in sadness.
　Love's holy light
　Shall banish night,
And change the gloom to gladness!

　Love cannot die!
　'Tis Deity!
'Tis bliss, pure, bright, supernal
　Though worlds shall fall
　To ruin, – all.
Yes, all of Love's eternal!

Alfred Gibbs Campbell (1826–1884)

20 DECEMBER

Lines to a Lady

It is not, Celia, in our power
To say how long our love will last;
It may be we within this hour
May lose those joys we now do taste;
   The blessèd, who immortal be,
   From change in love are only free.

Then since we mortal lovers are,
Ask not how long our love will last;
But while it does, let us take care
Each minute be with pleasure past:
   Were it not madness to deny
   To live, because we're sure to die?

George Etherege (c.1636–c.1692)

21 DECEMBER

Echoes of Love's House

Love gives every gift whereby we long to live
'Love takes every gift, and nothing back doth give.'

Love unlocks the lips that else were ever dumb:
'Love locks up the lips whence all things good might come.'

Love makes clear the eyes that else would never see:
'Love makes blind the eyes to all but me and thee.'

Love turns life to joy till nought is left to gain:
'Love turns life to woe till hope is nought and vain.'

Love, who changest all, change me nevermore!
'Love, who changest all, change my sorrow sore!'

Love burns up the world to changeless heaven and blest,
'Love burns up the world to a void of all unrest.'

And there we twain are left, and no more work we need:
'And I am left alone, and who my work shall heed?'

Ah! I praise thee, Love, for utter joyance won!
'And is my praise nought worth for all my life undone?'

William Morris (1834–1896)

22 DECEMBER

Ah, Eros doth not always smite

Ah, Eros doth not always smite
With cruel, shining dart,
Whose bitter point with sudden might
Rends the unhappy heart –

O'er it sometimes the boy will deign
Sweep the shaft's feathered end;
And friendship rises without pain
Where the white plumes descend.

Katherine Bradley (1846–1914) and Edith Cooper (1862–1913)
writing as
Michael Field

23 DECEMBER

Ballad

O sigh no more, love, sigh no more
Nor pine for earthly treasure
Who fears a shipwreck on the shore
Or meets despair with pleasure

Let not again our wants our troubles prove
Although 'tis winter weather
Nor singly strive with what our love
Can better brave together

Thy love is proved thy worth is such
It cannot fail to bless me
If I lose thee I can't be rich
Nor poor if I possess thee

John Clare (1793–1864)

24 DECEMBER

If I Could Tell You

Time will say nothing but I told you so,
Time only knows the price we have to pay;
If I could tell you I would let you know.

If we should weep when clowns put on their show,
If we should stumble when musicians play,
Time will say nothing but I told you so.

There are no fortunes to be told, although,
Because I love you more than I can say,
If I could tell you I would let you know.

The winds must come from somewhere when they blow,
There must be reasons why the leaves decay;
Time will say nothing but I told you so.

Perhaps the roses really want to grow,
The vision seriously intends to stay;
If I could tell you I would let you know.

Suppose the lions all get up and go,
And all the brooks and soldiers run away;
Will Time say nothing but I told you so?
If I could tell you I would let you know.

W. H. Auden (1907–1973)

25 DECEMBER

Christmastide

Love came down at Christmas,
  Love all lovely, Love Divine;
Love was born at Christmas,
  Star and Angels gave the sign.

Worship we the Godhead,
  Love Incarnate, Love Divine;
Worship we our Jesus:
  But wherewith for sacred sign?

Love shall be our token,
  Love be yours and love be mine,
Love to God and all men,
  Love for plea and gift and sign.

Christina Rossetti (1830–1894)

26 DECEMBER

The Face that Launched a Thousand Ships
FROM *DOCTOR FAUSTUS*, ACT V, SCENE I

Enter Helen
Faustus:
Was this the face that launch'd a thousand ships,
And burnt the topless towers of Ilium?
Sweet Helen, make me immortal with a kiss:
Her lips suck forth my soul, see where it flies.
Come, Helen, come, give me my soul again.
Here will I dwell, for heaven is in these lips,
And all is dross that is not Helena.
I will be Paris, and for love of thee,
Instead of Troy, shall Wittenberg be sack'd,
And I will combat with weak Menelaus,
And wear thy colours on my plumed crest.
Yea, I will wound Achilles in the heel,
And then return to Helen for a kiss.
O, thou art fairer than the evening's air
Clad in the beauty of a thousand stars.
Brighter art thou than flaming Jupiter,
When he appear'd to hapless Semele:
More lovely than the monarch of the sky,
In wanton Arethusa's azur'd arms;
And none but thou shalt be my paramour.

Christopher Marlowe (1564–1593)

27 DECEMBER

To Helen

Helen, thy beauty is to me
   Like those Nicèan barks of yore,
That gently, o'er a perfumed sea,
   The weary, way-worn wanderer bore
   To his own native shore.

On desperate seas long wont to roam,
   Thy hyacinth hair, thy classic face,
Thy Naiad airs have brought me home
   To the glory that was Greece,
And the grandeur that was Rome.

Lo! in yon brilliant window-niche
   How statue-like I see thee stand,
   The agate lamp within thy hand!
Ah, Psyche, from the regions which
   Are Holy-Land!

Edgar Allan Poe (1809–1849)

28 December

A Marriage Ring

The ring, so worn as you behold,
So thin, so pale, is yet of gold:
The passion such it was to prove;
Worn with life's care, love yet was love.

George Crabbe (1754–1832)

29 december

Not Anyone Who Says

Not anyone who says, 'I'm going to be
   careful and smart in matters of love,'
who says, 'I'm going to choose slowly,'
but only those lovers who didn't choose at all
but were, as it were, chosen
by something invisible and powerful and uncontrollable
and beautiful and possibly even
unsuitable –
only those know what I'm talking about
in this talking about love.

Mary Oliver (1935–2019)

30 DECEMBER

To [Charles Burney]

Oh, Author of my being! – far more dear
   To me than light, than nourishment, or rest,
Hygeia's blessings, Rapture's burning tear,
   Or the life-blood that mantles in my breast!

If in my heart the love of Virtue glows,
   'Twas planted there by an unerring rule;
From thy example the pure flame arose,
   Thy life, my precept – thy good works, my school.

Could my weak powers thy numerous virtues trace,
   By filial love each fear should be repressed,
The blush of Incapacity I'd chace,
   And stand, Recorder of thy worth, confessed:

But since my niggard stars that gift refuse,
   Concealment is the only boon I claim;
Obscure be still the unsuccessful Muse,
   Who cannot raise, but would not sink, thy fame.

Oh! of my life at once the source and joy!
   If e'er thy eyes these feeble lines survey,
Let not their folly their intent destroy;
   Accept the tribute – but forget the lay.

Frances Burney (1752–1840)

31 DECEMBER

Love

So, the year's done with
   (*Love me for ever!*)
All March begun with,
   April's endeavour;
May-wreaths that bound me
   June needs must sever;
Now snows fall round me,
   Quenching June's fever –
(*Love me for ever!*)

Robert Browning (1812–1889)

Index of First Lines

'A face that should content me wonders well' 26
'A glimpse through an interstice caught' 78
'A man who would woo a fair maid' 240–1
'A Scholar first my Love implor'd' 334
'Ae fond kiss, and then we sever!' 357
'Ah, Eros does not always smite' 438
'Ah! what is love? It is a pretty thing' 319–20
'Alas, for the blight of my fancies!' 55–6
'Alas! madame, for stelyng of a kisse' 370
'Alas my love ye do me wrong' 162
'All day my sheep have mingled with yours.
  They strayed' 316
'All thoughts, all passions, all delights' 212
'Ancient person, for whom I' 405
'And in a launde, upon an hille of floures' 63
'And you, Helen, what should I give you?' 364
'Ann thou art divinely fair' 152
'Are you the new person drawn toward me?' 140
'Arise, my trusty page' 163
'As Cloris full of harmless thought' 294
'As close as you your weding kept' 36
'As I walked out one evening' 221
'Ask me no more, my Truth to prove' 414
'Ask me no more where Jove bestows' 409
'Ask not the Cause why sullen Spring 117
'At nine in the morning there passed a church' 283

'Between the brown hands of a server-lad' 101
'Between the dusk of a summer night' 205
'Blest bridegroom, this day of matrimony' 54
'Bright star, would I were stedfast as thou art' 343
'Busie old foole, unruly Sunne' 245–6

449

'Come' 59
'Come, be my Valentine!' 72
'Come, come,' said Tom's father, 'at your time of life' 133
'Come in the evening, or come in the morning' 203
'Come, Let us roam the night together' 263
'Come live with me and be my love' 291
'Come, Madam, come, all rest my powers defie' 281
'Come, my Celia, let us prove' 249
'Come now, my love, the moon is on the lake' 268
'Come to me in the silence of the night' 362

'Dear God, 'tis hard, so awful hard to lose' 52
'Dear Lady of the Cherries, cool, serene' 242
'Dear love, what thing of all the things that be' 116
'Dear things! we would not have you learn too much' 382
'Don't talk to me of love. I've had an earful' 218–19
'Don't think' 284
'Drink to me only with thine eyes' 355

'Eight o'clock bells are ringing' 100
'Eph. What Friendship is, ARDELIA shew' 50
'Evening falls on the smoky walls' 262
'Except for the body' 374
'Eyes, calm beside thee, (Lady could'st thou know!) 132

'Fair maiden when my love began' 216
'Falling out of love' 383
'Fast falls the snow, O lady mine' 70
'Faustus: Was this the face that launch'd a thousand ships' 442
'Filling her compact & delicious body' 21
'First time he kissed me, he but only kissed' 188
'Fresh spring the herald of loves mighty king' 124
'Friend, whose smile has come to be' 384–5
'From the Desert I come to thee' 171–2

'Gather ye Rose-buds while ye may' 222
'Gentlest Air thou breath of Lovers' 358
'Give all to love' 286–7
'Glories, pleasures, pomps, delights, and ease' 68
'Go, lovely rose!' 217
'God with honour hang your head' 347
'Good night, love!' 337

'Had we but World enough, and Time' 61–2
'He first deceas'd, She for a little tri'd' 99
'He has married me with a ring, a ring of bright water' 296
'He'd been in the café since ten-thirty' 86–7
'Helen, thy beauty is to me' 443
'Here with a Loaf of Bread beneath the Bough' 381
'How do I love thee? Let me count the ways' 208
'How I do love to sit and dream' 274
'How ill doth he deserve a lover's name' 346
'How Love came in, I do not know' 359
'How many times do I love thee, dear?' 104
'How pleasant is love' 323
'How sweet I roam'd from field to field' 185
'How vilely 'twere to misdeserve' 80

'I am a flower' 123
'I am in love, meantime, you think, no doubt you would think so' 401
'I am not yours, not lost in you' 37
'I am the rose of Sharon' 109–10
'I bring you with reverent hands' 19
'I can write no stately proem' 371
'I cannot choose but think upon the time' 399
'I cannot see your face' 184
'i carry your heart with me(i carry it in)' 39
'I cry your mercy, pity – love – aye, love!' 388
'I envy not in any moods' 410

'I have been here before' 308
'I have learned not to worry about love' 233
'I have no Life but this' 260
'I joy to see how in your drawen work' 168
'I kissed them in fancy as I came' 350
'I know someone who kisses the way' 238
'I like to get off with people' 135
'I live in you, you live in me' 204
'I looked here' 293
'I love her with the seasons, with the winds' 48
'I love you with my life – 'tis so I love you' 105
'I loved thee from the earliest dawn' 13
'I loved you first: but afterwards your love' 392
'I met Louisa in the shade' 169
'I must not think of thee, and, tired yet strong' 372
'I must tell you, my dear' 325
'I played with you 'mid cowslips blowing' 92–3
'I pray thee leave, love me no more' 373
'I really must confess, my dear' 257–8
'I sat with Love upon a woodside well' 166
'I should have thought' 253–4
'I stood and saw my Mistress dance' 174
'I think I should have loved you presently' 404
'I want you and you are not here. I pause' 243
'I whispered, 'I am too young' 387
'I will not let you say a Woman's part' 22–3
'I will not love thee more' 289
'I will take your heart' 71
'I wish I could remember that first day' 18
'I wonder by my troth, what thou, and I' 131
'If a large hart, joynd with a noble mind' 314–15
'If all the world and love were young' 292
'If ever two were one, then surely we' 143
'If I could make a love quilt' 400
'If I were loved as I desire to be' 91
'If life were but a dream, my Love' 113

'If love the virgin's heart invade' 368
'If love were what the rose is' 348–9
'If to be absent were to be' 317
'If you loved me I could trust you to your fancy's furthest bound' 369
'I'll range around the shady bowers' 250–1
'I'm a broken-hearted Gardener, and don't know what to do' 161
'In summer's heat and mid-time of the day' 232
'In this early dancing of a new day' 194
'In the wild soft summer darkness' 220
'is love an abstract noun' 112
'Is love so prone to change and rot' 210
'It chanced that Cupid on a season' 415
'It is not, Celia, in our power' 436
'It is summer, and we are in a house' 290
'It matters not its history, love has wings' 96
'It sheds a shy solemnity' 180
'It was a bowl of roses' 236
'It was a lover and his lass' 145
'It was many and many a year ago' 114–15
'It was your lightness that drew me' 159
'It was your way, my dear' 16

'Jenny kissed me when we met' 118
'John Anderson my jo, John' 90
'Juliet: My bounty is as boundless as the sea' 332

'Last night, ah, yesternight, betwixt her lips and mine' 237
'Lay your sleeping head, my love' 306–7
'Learn to know' 329
'Leave me, O Love, which reachest but to dust' 351
'Lend me, a little while, the key' 34
'Let me not to the marriage of true minds' 12
'Let us not speak, for the love we bear one another' 248

'Life an enfranchised bird, who wildly springs' 231
'Light, so low upon earth' 269
'Like the touch of rain she was' 43
'Looking up at the stars, I know quite well' 79
'Love and the gentle heart are one same thing' 426
'Love bade me welcome. Yet my soul drew back' 298
'Love came down at Christmas' 441
'Love for such a cherry lip' 390
'Love gives every gift whereby we long to live' 437
'Love guards the roses of thy lips' 285
'Love hath a language of his own' 33
'Love in Fantastique Triumph satt' 69
'Love in her Sunny Eyes does basking play' 255
'Love is a startled bird that sings' 360
'Love is a wild wonder' 344
'Love is enough. Let us not ask for gold' 176–7
'Love is enough: though the World be a-waning' 322
'Love is like a lamb, and love is like a lion' 17
'Love is not all: it is not meat or drink' 206
'Love Love to-day, my dear' 98
'Love me – and I will give into your hands' 199
'Love me as I love thee. O double sweet!' 430
'Love still is Love, and doeth all things well' 278
'Love, that liveth, and raigneth in my thought' 58
'Love, the delight of all well-thinking minds' 149
'Love understands the mystery, whereof' 178
'Love without hope, as when the young bird-catcher' 198
'Lovely fairy! Charming sprite' 352
'Loving in truth, and fain in verse my love to show' 95

'Madam, I hope you think it's true' 147–8
'may i feel said he' 397–8
'me think about her when sun rises' 354
'Me thinks I see faire Virtue readie stand' 234–5
'Miss. J. Hunter Dunn, Miss J. Hunter Dunn' 279–80
'Mixed marriages do have their advantages' 336

'Morning drops down' 379
'Mother says, 'Be in no hurry'' 65–6
'Music, when soft voices die' 393
'My attention was directed by something said beside me' 422
'My dear, true wife' 435
'My delight and thy delight' 297
'My dog (the trustiest of his kind)' 261
'My father is deceas'd. Come, Gaveston' 20
'My Love is of a birth as rare' 136–7
'My love is of comely height and straight' 160
'My luve is like a red, red rose' 200
'My mistress' eyes are nothing like the sun' 304
'My mother loved my father' 276
'My true love hath my hart, and I have his' 134

'Never seek to tell thy love' 77
'Never think she loves him wholly' 389
'no' 85
'No, no, for my virginity' 295
'No one so much as you' 195
'Not anyone who says, I'm going to be' 445
'Not caring to observe the wind' 31
'Now sleeps the crimson petal, now the white' 264

'O gentle Love, ungentle for thy deed' 365
'O hurry where by water among the trees' 345
'O sign no more, love, sign no more' 439
'O Sweetheart, hear you' 224
'O Western wind, when wilt thou blow' 53
'O what can ail thee, knight-at-arms' 366–7
'O what uphop't for sweet supply!' 142
'Of all the girls that are so smart' 432–3
'Oh, Author of my being! far more dear' 446
'Oh, can we love and live? Pray, let us die' 89
'Oh! Death will find me, long before I tire' 150

'Oh! had I that poetic lore' 299
'Oh, say not, my love, with that mortified air' 270
'Oh, the nights were dark and cold' 421
'Oh, when I was in love with you' 288
'Oh, where's the maid that I can love' 179
'On this lone island, whose unfruitful breast' 230
'On Waterloo Bridge where we said our goodbyes' 106
'Once in the world's first prime' 282
'One day I wrote her name upon the strand' 202
'One innocent spring' 175
'Only a dying horse! pull off the gear' 25
'Our world is very little in the sky' 144
'Out of the dusk of distant woods' 129
'Out of this love' 209
'Out upon it, I have loved' 126
'Outside the sky is light with stars' 127

'Pack, clouds away! and welcome day!' 102
'Polly: Can love be controlled by advice?' 24

'River, be their teacher' 186

'Say over again, and yet once over gain' 125
'See how the pair of billing doves' 342
'Seventeen years ago you said' 182
'Shall I compare thee to a summer's day' 228
'She brings that breath, and music too' 138
'She dwelt among the untrodden ways' 139
'She is most fair' 428–9
'She is not fair to outward view' 239
'She stood breast high amid the corn' 324
'She tells her love while half asleep' 14
'She walks in beauty, like the night' 153
'She, who so long has lain' 167
'She wore a 'terra-cotta' dress' 310
'Side by side, their faces blurred' 27–8

'Sighing, and sadly sitting by my Love' 407
'Since there's no help, come let us kiss and part' 187
'Sing in me now you words' 41
'So Miss Myrtle is going to marry' 311–13
'So, the year's done with' 447
'So, we'll go no more a roving' 321
'Soft breezes blow and swiftly show' 223
'Some men never think of it' 213
'somewhere i have never travelled, gladly beyond' 181
'Somewhere on the other side of this wide night' 406
'Soon we both shall share a stone' 51
'Stars are the nipples' 32
'Stay near to me and I'll stay near to you' 151
'Strephon kissed me in the spring' 420
'Sweet are the Charms of her I love' 107
'Sweet mother, I can't take shuttle in hand' 396
'Sweetheart, is this the last of all our posies' 272

'Take this kiss upon the brow!' 35
'Talking in bed ought to be easiest' 318
'Tell – dear Aminta, now 'tis over' 128
'Tell me it was for the hunger' 94
'Tell me no more of constancy' 164
'That his eyebrows were false – that his hair' 122
'That I did always love' 30
'That time of year thou mayst in me behold' 378
'The day he moved out was terrible' 363
'The fountains mingle with the river' 277
'The full September moon sheds floods of light' 305
'The gray of the sea, and the gray of the sky' 333
'The grey sea and the long black land' 256
'The highway is full of big cars' 76
'The lark now leaves his watery nest' 211
'The life that I have' 423
'The lilies clustered fair and tall' 192
'The love you dare but look I find' 424

'The lover for shamefastnesse hideth his desire within his faithfull hart' 57
'The lowest trees have tops, the ant her gall' 386
'The merchant, to secure his treasure' 425
'The morning breaks like a pomegranate' 74–5
'The Muses found young Love one day' 330
'The night has a thousand eyes' 170
'The ring, so worn as you behold' 444
'The sea is calm tonight' 214–15
'The sun has burst the sky' 157
'There are two births, the one when light' 173
'There lies a photograph of you' 356
'There on the top of the down' 201
'There's a tanker on the horizon' 44
'They are agitated' 331
'They were so very sad' 130
'Things base and vile, holding no quantity' 207
'This book, this page, this harebell laid to rest' 271
'This love of nature, that allures to take' 328
'This poring over your Grand Cyrus' 64
'Thou hast loved and thou hast suffer'd' 29
'Time now makes a new beginning 146
'Time will say nothing but I told you so' 440
''Tis the human touch in this world that counts' 49
'To any Phillis or Chloe' 88
'To lose thee – sweeter than to gain' 326
'To make a final conquest of all me' 403
'To whom I owe the leaping delight' 165
'Trusty, dusky, vivid, true' 252
'Twice or thrice had I loved thee' 259
'Two separate divided silences' 275
'Two wedded lovers watched the rising moon' 193

'Under the lime tree, on the daisied ground' 196–7
'Unto the boundless ocean of thy beauty' 434

'We climbed one morning to the sunny height' 300
'We two that planets erst had been' 67
'Werther had a love for Charlotte' 111
'What ecstasies her bosom fire!' 335
'What lips my lips have kissed, and where, and why' 416
'When as in silks my Julia goes' 273
'When as the rye reach to the chin' 309
'When autumn winds are on the hill' 402
'When did it happen?' 141
'When I am dead, my dearest' 380
'When I am sad and weary' 338
'When I heard at the close of the day how my name had been' 408
'When I was one-and-twenty' 229
'When, in disgrace with fortune and men's eyes' 156
'When love beckons to you, follow him' 327
'When Love had shaped this world, this great fair wight' 40
'When lovely woman stoops to folly' 38
'When she rises in the morning' 247
'When we two walked in Lent' 103
'While love is unfashionable' 60
'Whil'st Alexis lay prest' 244
'Who'er she be' 353
'Why is my verse so barren of new pride' 84
'Why should you swear I am forsworn' 42
'Why so pale and wan fond lover?' 361
'Wild Nights – Wild Nights!' 97
'Wind whines and whines the shingle' 391
'Winds, whisper gently whilst she sleeps' 73
'Wine comes in at the mouth' 431
'With fruit and flowers the board is deckt' 108
'With thee conversing I forget all time' 158
'Wou'd you wish to keep your lover' 15

'Ye cats that at midnight spit love at each other' 417
'Ye Virgins that from Cupids tentes' 418–19
'You won't believe it. Perhaps you're too prosaic' 427
'Your hands, my dear, adorable' 394–5
'Your yën two wol slee me sodenly' 183

Index of Poets

A

Agard, John 186, 336
Allen, Elizabeth Akers 384–5
Andrewes, Lancelot, Bishop of Winchester 72
Angelou, Maya 76, 175
Armitage, Simon 271
Arnold, Matthew 214–15
Auden, W. H. 79, 221, 306–7, 440
Austin, David 51, 209

B

Barnes, William 160
Barnfield, Richard 407
Barrett Browning, Elizabeth 125, 188, 208
Bateman, Meg 159
Beddoes, Thomas Lovell 104
Behn, Aphra 69
Berryman, John 21
Betjeman, John 248, 279–80
Bevington, L. S. 144
Bilston, Brian 112, 354
Binyon, Laurence 129
Blake, William 77, 185
Booth, Barton 107
Bourdillon, Francis William 170
Bradley, Katherine 48, 105, 438
Bradstreet, Anne 143
Bridges, Robert 297
Brooke, Rupert 150, 394–5
Browning, Robert 132, 256, 447
Burney, Frances 446
Burns, Robert 90, 200, 357
Byron, Lord George Gordon 153, 321

C

Cameron, Norman 316
Campbell, Alfred Gibbs 435
Campion, Thomas 142
Carew, Thomas 346, 409
Carey, Henry 250–1, 432–3
Cartwright, William 173
Cather, Willa 116, 289, 330
Cavafy, Constantine 86–7, 130, 422
Cavendish, William, Duke of Newcastle 89
Chappell, Henry 25
Chaucer, Geoffrey 63, 183
Clare, John 216, 439
Clough, Arthur Hugh 401
Coleridge, Hartley 239
Coleridge, Samuel Taylor 212
Collins, Mortimer 70
Cooper, Edith 48, 105, 438
Cope, Wendy 106, 213, 363
Cotton, Charles 73
Cowley, Abraham 255
Crabbe, George 444
Crane, Hart 180
Crane, Stephen 293
Crashaw, Richard 353
cummings, e.e. 39, 181, 397–8

D

Daniel, Samuel 434
Dante Alighieri 426
Davenant, Sir William 211
Davies, Sir John 40
Davies, W. H. 138, 274
Davis, Thomas O. 203
Dickinson, Emily 30, 97, 260, 326
Dixon, Sarah 128

Donne, John 131, 245–6, 259, 281
Doolittle, Hilda (H. D.) 253–4
Dowson, Ernest 237
Drayton, Michael 187, 373
Dryden, John 117, 244
Dubois, Lady Dorothy 334
Dufferin, Lady Helen 311–13
Duffy, Carol Ann 243, 406
Dunbar, Paul Laurence 113, 333
Dunn, Douglas 204, 290, 427
Dyer, Sir Edward 386
Dyer, Lady Katherine 314–15

E
Egerton, Sarah Fyge 323
Eliot, George 399
Eliot, T. S. 165
Emerson, Ralph Waldo 286–7
Etherege, George 436

F
Fenton, James 151, 218–19
Field, Michael 48, 105, 438
Field, Rachel 360
Finch, Anne 50, 358
Flatman, Thomas 417
Flecker, James Elroy 262, 356
Ford, John 68
Free, Spencer Michael 49
Fuller, John 146

G
Gay, John 24, 261, 335, 368
Gibran, Kahlil 327
Gilbert, W. S. 240–1
Giovanni, Nikki 123, 400

Goldsmith, Oliver 38
Goodison, Lorna 276
Graves, Robert 14, 198
Greene, Robert 319–20
Greville, Fulke, Lord Brooke 149
Gurney, Ivor 41

H
H. D. (Hilda Doolittle) 253–4
Hardy, Thomas 16, 283, 310, 350
Heine, Heinrich 163
Hemans, Felicia 29
Henley, W. E. 205, 236
Herbert, George 298
Herrick, Robert 222, 273, 359
Heywood, Thomas 102
Hood, Thomas 324
Hopkins, Gerard Manley 347, 430
Horton, George Moses 13
Housman, A. E. 229, 288
Hughes, Langston 71, 263, 344
Hunt, Leigh 118

J
Jonson, Ben 249, 355
Joseph, Jenny 157
Joyce, James 224, 391

K
kaur, rupi 85
Keats, John 343, 366–7, 388
Kemble, Frances Anne 337
al-Khayyám, Omar ibn Ibrahim 381
The King James Bible 109–10

L

Landen, Letitia Elizabeth (L.E.L.) 96
Lanyer, Aemilia 234–5
Larkin, Philip 27–8, 318
Lawrence, D. H. 74–5, 247
Leapor, Mary 147–8
L.E.L. 96
Levy, Amy 108, 167
Lodge, Thomas 285
Lovelace, Richard 42, 317
Lowell, Amy 184

M

McClellan, George Marion 305
MacDonald, George 59
Madan, Judith 352
Mansfield, Katherine 127
Marks, Leo 423
Marlowe, Christopher 20, 291, 442
Marvell, Andrew 61–2, 136–7, 403
Massey, Gerald 382
Meredith, George 193, 328
Mew, Charlotte 34, 98, 182, 272
Meynell, Alice 372
Middleton, Thomas 17, 390
Millay, Edna St Vincent 206, 404, 416
Millicheap, Paul 112, 354
Milton, John 158
Mitchell, Adrian 338
Monck, Mary 64
Montagu, Lady Mary Wortley 342
Moore, Thomas 33, 88, 133
Morris, William 322, 437

N

Naden, Constance 55–6
Nelson, Alice Dunbar 52, 223, 257–8
Nesbit, E. 369, 421
Nichols, Grace 32
Norton, Caroline 231

O

Oliver, Mary 141, 194, 238, 374, 445
Osgood, Frances Sargent 122
Ovid 232
Owen, Wilfred 101

P

Patmore, Coventry 80
Peacock, Thomas Love 92–3
Peele, George 309, 365
Petraca, Francesco (Petrarch) 57, 58
Piercy, Marge 284, 383
Poe, Edgar Allan 35, 114–15, 443
Prior, Matthew 295, 425
Probyn, May 325
Procter, Adelaide 22–3

R

Raine, Kathleen 296
Raleigh, Sir Walter 292
Reeve, Clara 15
Robinson, A. Mary F. 300
Rossetti, Christina 18, 178, 210, 278, 362, 380, 392, 441
Rossetti, D. G. 166, 275, 308

S

Sansom, Martha 424
Sappho 54, 396
Scott, Sir Walter 270, 415

Shakespeare, William 12, 84, 145, 156, 207, 228, 304, 332, 378
Shelley, Percy Bysshe 277, 393
Shirley, James 174
Sidney, Sir Philip 95, 134, 351
Smith, Charlotte 230
Smith, Stevie 135
Spenser, Edmund 124, 168, 202
Stevenson, Robert Louis 252
Suckling, Sir John 126, 361
Swinburne, Algernon Charles 348–9
Synková, Jana 44, 329, 379

T
Taylor, Bayard 171–2
Teasdale, Sara 37, 220, 389, 420
Tennyson, Lord Alfred 91, 201, 264, 269, 410
Thackeray, W. M. 111
Thaxter, Celia 192
Thomas, Edward 43, 103, 195, 364, 428–9
Thoreau, Henry David 67
Tollet, Elizabeth 414
Tomoana, Paraire 'Friday' Henare 331

V
Victorian street ballad 161
Vogelweide, Walther von der 196–7
Vuong, Ocean 94

W
Walden, Islay 179
Walker, Alice 60, 233
Waller, Edmund 31, 217
Wavell, A. P. 242
Webb, Mary 199, 402
Whitfield, James Monroe 299

Whitman, Albery Allson 268
Whitman, Walt 78, 140, 408
Whitney, Isabella 36, 418–19
Wilcox, Ella Wheeler 65–6, 176–7, 282
Wilde, Oscar 371
Wilmot, John, Lord Rochester 164, 294, 405
Wordsworth, William 139, 169
Wotton, Sir Henry 99
Wyatt, Sir Thomas 26, 370

Y

Yeats, W. B. 19, 345, 387, 431

Sources

W. John Agard, 'Mixed Marriages' and 'Nuptials' from We Brits (2006) and Travel Light Travel Dark (2013). Reproduced with permission of Bloodaxe Books. www.bloodaxebooks.co

Maya Angelou, 'Now Long Ago' and 'Come. And Be My Baby' from Oh Pray My Wings Are Gonna Fit Me Well (1975) Caged Bird Legacy, LLC. Used by permission of Random House, an imprint and division of Penguin Random House LLC. All rights reserved. Maya Angelou: The Complete Poetry, Little Brown Book Group Limited, reproduced with permission of the Licensor through PLSclear.

W. H. Auden, 'If I Could Tell You', 'As I Walked Out One Evening', 'Lullaby' and 'the More Loving One' from Collected Shorter Poems 1927-1957 (1966). Copyright © 1966 by The Estate of W.H. Auden. Reprinted by permission of Curtis Brown, Ltd. All rights reserved.

David Austin, 'Some Casual Passer-by' and 'Out of this Love', © David Austin, Enitharmon Press.

Meg Bateman, 'Lightness', © Meg Bateman, Polygon Edinburgh.

John Berryman, 'The Dream Songs, Part I, 4, Filling her compact & delicious body', © John Berryman, Faber & Faber.

John Betjeman, 'A Subalterns Love-song' and 'In a Bath Teashop', © John Betjeman, John Murray / Hodder and Stoughton, Hachette.

Brian Bilston, 'The Caveman's Lament' and 'Love in the Age of Google', @ Brian Bilston, Pan Macmillan.

Constantine Cavafy, 'At the entrance of the café', 'Two young men, 23 to 24 years old' and 'They are changed by Time' from The Collected Poems: With Parallel Greek (2008), Oxford Univerity Press, Oxford Publishing Limited, reproduced with permission of the Licensor through PLSclear.

Wendy Cope, 'After Lunch', 'Flowers' and 'Loss', @ Wendy Cope, Faber & Faber.

e. e. cummings 'i carry your heart with me(i carry it in'. Copyright 1952, (c) 1980, 1991 by the Trustees for the E. E. Cummings Trust, 'may i feel said he'. Copyright 1935, (c) 1963, 1991 by the Trustees for the E. E. Cummings Trust. Copyright (c) 1978 by George James Firmage, 'somewhere i have never travelled,gladly beyond'. Copyright 1931, (c) 1959, 1991 by the Trustees for the E. E. Cummings Trust. Copyright (c) 1979 by George James Firmage, from COMPLETE POEMS: 1904-1962 by E. E. Cummings, edited by George J. Firmage. Used by permission of Liveright Publishing Corporation.

Hilda Doolittle, 'At Baia' from Collected Poems, 1912-1944 (1982), copyright given by The Estate of Hilda Doolittle. Reprinted by permission of New Directions Publishing Corp, and Carcanet Press Limited.

Carol Ann Duffy, 'Miles Away' and 'Words, Wide Night', @ Carol Ann Duffy, Penguin Random House Ltd.

Douglas Dunn, 'You', 'Love Poem' and 'Modern Love', @ Douglas Dunn, Faber & Faber.

T. S. Eliot, 'A Dedication to My Wife', © T. S. Eliot, Faber & Faber.

James Fenton, 'Hinterhof' and 'In Paris with You', © James Fenton, Faber & Faber.

John Fuller, 'Time Now Makes a New Beginning from Birth Bells for Louisa', © John Fuller, Chatto and Windus.

Nikki Giovanni, 'Some Call it Love' and 'Love in all Colours', © Nikki Giovanni, Harper Collins.

Lorna Goodison, 'For My Mother (May I Inherit Half Her Strength)' from Quartet of Poems (1993) published by Longman. Permission kindly given by Lorna Goodison.

Robert Graves, 'Love Without Hope' and 'She Tells Her Love While Half Asleep' from Complete Poems Vol 1 (1986). Reproduced by permission of Carcanet Press Limited.

Langston Hughes, 'Harlem Night Song', 'Love, Love is a wild wonder' and 'To Artina' from Selected Poems (2020), reprinted by permission of Profile Books Ltd.

Jenny Joseph, 'The Sun has Burst the Sky' from Rose in Afternoon and Other Poems (1973), Aldine Press, reprinted by permission of Johnson & Alcock Ltd.

Rupi Kaur, 'no, it won't be love at first sight', © Rupi Kaur, Andrews McMeel Publishing.

Philip Larkin, 'An Arundel Tomb' and 'Talking in Bed', © Philip Larkin, Faber & Faber.

Leo Marks, 'The Life That I Have', © Leo Marks, Harper Collins.

Adrian Mitchell, 'Celia Celia' from For Beauty Douglas, Collected Poems 1953-1979 (1982). Permission given by United Agents and the Adrian Mitchell Estate.

Grace Nichols, 'On Stars', © Grace Nichols, Curtis Brown.

Mary Oliver, 'When Did It Happen?', 'I Know Someone', 'This and That', 'Except for the Body' and 'Not Anyone Who Says', © Mary Oliver, Corsair Poetry, Hachette.

Marge Piercy, 'Girl in white' and 'Erasure' from Circles on the Water by Marge Piercy, copyright © 1982 by Middlemarsh, Inc. Used by permission of Alfred A. Knopf, an imprint of the Knopf Doubleday Publishing Group, a division of Penguin Random House LLC. All rights reserved.

Kathleen Raine, 'The Ring from The Marriage', © Kathleen Raine, George Allen & Unwin.

Sappho, 'Sweet Mother' and 'Blest bridegroom', Penguin Random House Ltd.

Stevie Smith, 'Conviction (IV) I like to get off with people', © Stevie Smith, Faber & Faber.

Jana Synková, 'Ships Passing', 'Eye of the Beholder', and 'Play-acting', reproduced with kind permission of Jana Synková.

Ocean Vuong, 'On Earth We're Briefly Gorgeous', © Ocean Vuong, Copper Canyon Press.

Alice Walker, 'New Face' and 'While Love is Unfashionable', © Alice Walker, Joy Harris Literary Agency.

Batsford is committed to respecting the intellectual property rights of others. We have taken all reasonable efforts to ensure that the reproduction of all contents on these pages is done with the full consent of the copyright owners. If you are aware of unintentional omissions, please contact the company directly so that any necessary corrections may be made for future editions.

Editor's Acknowledgements

As always my first thanks goes to Hatchards, at Piccadilly, St Pancras and Cheltenham for looking after my books so well.

Thanks to Julie Apps, Sally Hughes and Chris Kelly for suggestions and last, but definitely not least, to Nicola Newman and Rebecca Armstrong, my wonderful editors and everyone at Batsford who helps with these anthologies.

About the Editor

Jane McMorland Hunter has compiled anthologies for Batsford and the National Trust including collections on gardening, nature, friendship, London, England and the First World War. She has also worked as a gardener, potter and quilter, writes gardening, nature, cookery and craft books and works at Hatchards Bookshop in Piccadilly. She was brought up in the country but now lives happily in London in a house overflowing with books and a small garden overflowing with plants.